HOW TO PROFIT FROM THE FALLING DOLLAR

by

Cecil Robles

authorHOUSE®

AuthorHouse™
1663 Liberty Drive, Suite 200
Bloomington, IN 47403
www.authorhouse.com
Phone: 1-800-839-8640

First published by AuthorHouse 5/21/2007

ISBN: 978-1-4343-1103-0 (e)
ISBN: 978-1-4343-1101-6 (sc)
ISBN: 978-1-4343-1102-3 (hc)

Library of Congress Control Number: 2007903216

Printed in the United States of America
Bloomington, Indiana

This book is printed on acid-free paper.

TABLE OF CONTENTS

ACKNOWLEDGMENTS

To my Lord and Savior Jesus Christ;
My wife Kricie for all her support;
and John Vasquez my associate.

INTRODUCTION

By looking at the title of this book you may be saying to yourself, "This guy is really pessimistic about our economy." That couldn't be further from the truth. I want our economy to flourish just like most Americans. I am an optimist to the core. I believe there are more great opportunities in our nation than at any other time in history to those that will pursue them.

However, the bottom line is that our nation is in some serious trouble because we refuse to straighten up our act. For many the American Dream has become the American nightmare. We are sacrificing our future for an immediate gratification.

We as a nation need to wake up to the facts about our economic situation and do something about it. If we just stand by on the sidelines as spectators we will not make a difference. It really isn't right to simply pass the buck on to the next generation.

With that said, let me say that this book does not have all the answers. But then again I haven't read a financial book yet that does. My goal here is to show you how I believe we got to where we are today, where I think we are going and how you can position yourself for it.

The contents of this book are not meant to make you so fearful about the future that you don't do anything about it. However, sometimes fear is the greatest motivator for gain, so as you read learn to channel that emotion toward the solution. Read this book with an open mind and I believe you will find it to be very educational and helpful in your investment strategies.

CHAPTER 1

The Rise and Fall of the Empires

Throughout history we have seen the rise of many great empires: the Chinese, the Greeks, the Romans, the Spanish, the French, and the British, to name the most prominent and well known. Without exception the fall of every empire has occurred as well.

When an empire is born all look to see how this one will differ from the previous one. The empire starts off strong and prosperous and all say that destruction and ruin can never come, only to find that after the empire reaches its pinnacle the fall is with much more force and destruction than the rise. Maybe you have heard the saying, "The bigger they are the harder they fall," and this couldn't ring more true than in respect to the great empires our world has seen.

The way every empire is born is from the ashes of a previous empire. Every living thing is born from another living thing. Just as every human born has some resemblance to its parents so does every empire have a link to its foregoer. However this is not quite true about the United States. The foregoer of the United States was the British Empire and yet we see little resemblance between the system of imperial finance in the United States and the British

Empire. However, there is a slight family resemblance in the Spanish Colonial Empire.

During the Spanish Empire, Spain sent ships armed with provisions, soldiers, and colonial administrators. These ships returned to their motherland filled with newfound riches. They returned with gold and silver. Which was a hard asset. Real money. It was very hard to counterfeit this kind of currency, and they couldn't just make more of it at the stroke of a pen. These newfound riches, however good they may have seemed, were in fact extremely fatal to the empire. Sometimes extreme wealth gotten without much hard work is the worst thing that could happen to an empire. This is what took place in the case of Spain. They spent money without really earning it and they consumed more than they could produce. When the real money began to dry up they found that they were really poor, not rich.

So it is with America, except our case is worse. Our nation is nurtured by foreign wealth just like Spain was, excluding the real money. Instead of gold and silver we operate a paper money society. However in our foreign dependence it isn't even paper money that is transferred—it is electronically done. Nothing ever changes hands and there is nothing tangible backing the transaction. It is, simply put, a smoke and mirrors act. For instance if the U.S. Treasury makes a dollar bill it does not come with an additional dollar of savings or profit, and in most cases there is not even a real dollar. The gold from South and Central America was tangible and is still in circulation today.

With the First and Second World Wars also came the emergence of another great empire, The United States. During this period the United States was transformed from a mere republic into an empire. Now we have an interest in everything that happens in world politics and social issues, with our forces spanned across the globe. This is without a doubt the making of an empire.

In an empire, the way people think about their surroundings, the world, finance, and government changes. An imperial man begins to turn away from his home and immediate surroundings and begins to see the world as the big picture. They see all of the wrong that is taking place and think, "If I were running things they would be much different." Then he takes action and begins to play a bigger role in global affairs. Before long he becomes the main player and eventually earns the star role and all of the accolades and respect that come along with it.

Instead of enjoying their own land and efforts this newly born empire begins to look towards the efforts of foreign commerce, factories and fields to support it. Eventually this leads to the neglect of its own commerce and industry. While there is still the outflow of commands and proclamations from the center of the empire to the outer extremities, there is also an inflow. Such was the case with every empire since the beginning of time.

The major difference between a republic and an empire is that republics pay their own way and empires have foreign lands that pay their way. Such is the story with America. In 1952 almost 90 percent of the federal government's borrowing came from domestic investors. Most Americans religiously saved their money. Now in 2005 the tables have turned and instead of borrowing from home we borrow from overseas investors. In 1952 only 5 percent of treasury bonds were held by foreign hands, today the figure has changed to over 45 percent. At the same time domestic lending has been cut by 50 percent.

We get our automobiles from Japan and our electronics from Taiwan. Our clothes are now made in China and Malaysia. Most of our scientists and computer brains are coming from India. And the majority of the money it takes to keep it all running comes from the East.

Our Empire

As I have previously stated, America began her quest for empire status beginning with World Wars I and II. Since then America has seemed to step up its pace by engrossing itself in over 111 military actions and conflicts.

Our troops are scattered across the world in U.S. military bases found in over 120 countries. In addition to our military presence we also have scientists, contractors, consultants, advisors, engineers, intermediaries and functionaries throughout the globe. These people have been educated in American universities and are either on the payroll of the U.S. Government or U.S. companies that are linked to the government.

John Perkins, in his book called *Confessions of an Economic Hit Man*, (New York: Penguin, 2006) reveals the purpose and work of these people. A supervisor explained to him:

> *There were two primary objectives of my work. First I was to justify huge international loans that would funnel money back to MAIN (the consulting firm for whom he labored) and other U.S. companies such as Bechtel, Halliburton, Stone and Webster, and Brown and Root through massive engineering and construction projects. Second, I would work to bankrupt the countries that received those loans (after they had paid MAIN and other U.S. contractors, of course) so that they would be forever beholden to their creditors and so they would present easy targets when we needed favors, including military bases, UN votes, or access to oil and other natural resources.*

Although now we can see America with all of the trappings of an empire, our founders had mixed emotions about the status of empire. In fact they were all educated on the rise and fall of the Roman Empire and they vowed to not make the same mistakes.

But greed is a strong emotion that causes even the best of men to falter. Especially when coming from an imperial-minded society like Britain with its imperial purple on display.

So why does America have so many troops and foot soldiers scattered throughout the world? Why is it that America will spend more in a single year on defense than the rest of the world combined? At present America is the world's only superpower and we currently can be matched by no single nation militarily. Against what is she defending herself? This is the same thing that takes hold of every imperial power since the beginning of time. America has become the world's police because the world is her playground. She must now provide safety for the world. This is her job as she wears the imperial purple whether she wants to or not. So now America is the ruler of the world, but far from being the ruler of her own finances.

Everything about imperialism is attractive to man. The powers, money and fame that come along with an empire have attracted men since the beginning of time. This could not be truer than with America. Why is it that people outside of America are so attracted to America? Could it be that we are seen as the center of the empire? It is a place where there are more opportunities for success than any other place on the planet. People are attracted to America because of how we live: without a care in the world, and like everything is going to last forever. The big problem with this philosophy is that nothing lasts forever, especially great empires.

Of course there is not an empire yet that wanted to accept the idea that it could possibly come to an end. Somehow Americans seem to think of themselves as out of the ordinary and superior. However we have only been in existence for some 229 years. Nonetheless we tend to think of our civilization and our country as special and less likely to fall than other cultures that we think of as barbaric or ancient, pagan, or otherwise inferior.

Anthropologists, on the other hand, lend an opposing theory to the one aforementioned. They tell us after studying ancient civilizations that many of the fallen civilizations throughout history also thought they were superior to their neighbors or forebears. Just like Americans, few of their citizens believed that their society and economy could collapse. This is much like what we saw in the '99 technology stock collapse. Few investors thought that would happen, and the results were devastating and surprising to many people who had their life savings invested heavily in this area.

The Roman Empire lasted more than 1000 years, and yet we seem to have more confidence in our nation after only 229 years.

Recent scientific research points to the idea that our civilization is more fragile than we would like to think. According to Michael Shermer in a column he wrote for *Scientific American*, modern civilizations do not last as long as ancient civilizations. Among the twenty-eight most recent civilizations following the Roman Empire, the average life span is only 305 years. (Michael Shermer, Why ET Hasn't Called, *Scientific American*, August 2002)

One reason may be that modern civilizations are more complex. By this, we mean that they have a well-developed division of labor. In a well-developed division of labor most jobs require specialized skills and training. These modern civilizations also have a hierarchal leadership structure, with various levels of government and other social institutions. Modern civilizations are also more expensive to maintain because they require more natural resources to maintain their territories.

Civilizations tend to culminate around crisis. Often when a civilization is fragile the next crisis may be all that it takes to send them into an out of control spiral downward. After all just because a civilization has maintained its status for two or three hundred years does not mean that it will last forever. We do not have enough information about the future to say that a civilization will continue on infinitely. On the other hand we have plenty of history that shows us otherwise.

In his book, *The Collapse of Complex Societies*, Joseph Tainter gives us a reason why complex societies collapse. He explains that like other human endeavors, societies eventually suffer from diminishing returns. (Cambridge University Press, 1995)

For example, when we observe the Roman Empire we discover that they followed this same pattern. It started out when they wanted to conquer their neighbors to commandeer their grain production and labor to sustain Rome's own need. At first Rome was very successful with this approach and as a result they became very wealthy. There was, however, a downside to this new expansion. As they grew and conquered more territories, the need for a larger, more complex civil service and military force, education, public works, and social benefits grew exponentially. Of course every one of these expanding arms of the empire required more financing than ever before. The only option was to raise taxes and debase the currency. Eventually the taxes were so burdensome that landowners were forced to abandon their farms, which caused food production to fall. Soon the cost to conquer new territories exceeded the rewards. Then because of the imbalance that was already created in the economy Rome could no longer afford to defend the territories that it had conquered. Barbarians soon capitalized on the weaknesses and invaded the territories. The once great empire of Rome had fallen victim to its own tactics.

The bottom line is that our economy is very fragile. It is like walking on a tightrope without the use of a net. One little slip and we could fall to our demise. Unfortunately for us the complexity of our society and economy does not help much in making our economy more stable. I like to use the analogy of a four-legged stool to show the potential danger facing our economy.

A four-legged stool is only made stable by the legs that support it. If one leg breaks the stool becomes unstable and its use becomes obsolete until you fix it. If you knew a stool was broken and that you had the potential to fall if you sat in it would you sit? The answer is no. You wouldn't sit in it because of the potential to fall out of it which would do harm to your well-being.

The United States Empire is like the four-legged stool only instead of the legs we have real economic issues that we are currently facing. These issues are pushing us rapidly towards a changed America. In the chapters ahead you will read about the "broken legs" of our economy. The first and most likely trigger to a coming economic collapse is our severe debt. This debt spans nationwide on a private and public level. The "twin deficits" are looming factors in our debt situation. This may prove to be the reason for the demise of the dollar. It is by far the most dangerous problem and the one that could cause us to spin into a severe economic depression or a total economic collapse in the near future.

The second leg is a slowing economy caused by superficial gains in the '90s stock market bubble. This is more of a sign given to show the direction our economy is heading. With very little increase in technology and industrial production in recent years we are falling behind the rest of the world. Of course companies have learned how to spruce up their bottom lines to make things look attractive from the outside. The reality, however, is that American industry has fallen out of the race with the rest of the world and we are lagging a generation behind in most areas. Because of the shakiness of our economy and a falling dollar, companies are not willing to take new risks to expand and grow their businesses by seeking new customers and innovating their technology and services.

The third leg includes terrorism, energy prices, and inflation. These three are what I call sleeper disasters. These are things that could creep up on our economy at any moment and do serious damage. Terrorist attacks are unknown factors in the society that we live in today. The coming oil crisis is really a book in itself, however I will point out some serious threats that involve supply and demand which have the potential to send gas prices to $10 a gallon.

The fourth leg represents the growing economies of China and India. Currently China has not yet revalued their currency but when they do, watch out. A revaluation could cause an economic slowdown, even a recession in the United States.

All of these causes and effects have severe consequences on the value of the U.S. dollar and our economy. It could be a very short period of time before we see one of these crises manifest which would cause chaos and turmoil in America.

CHAPTER 2

America the Debt Empire

America is an empire, no doubt about that, but just what kind of empire is she? When the Roman Empire was at its financial peak around AD 36, there were over 700 million denarii in the treasury. This figure far exceeded any amount that had been there during the previous reign of Augustus. By the time of Nero's reign just a few short years later Rome was in severe debt. The trade deficit that she had with other states was running rampant with no end in sight. So Nero did what other rulers had done time and time again—clip the coinage (reduce the precious metal content). In the past 41 aurei had been minted from one pound of gold, but during this clipping of the coinage he reduced it to 45.

It was hard for Rome to maintain order throughout the empire because it was becoming so expensive to do so. Rome was now dependent on imported capital, imported soldiers, and imported goods. Sound familiar? This is exactly how America has become. Just like Rome America meets every new problem with more currency, only it is phony money.

The deception that has been produced by our economic status has played a big part in the changing mentality of many Americans. Up until the 1980s Americans saved around 10 percent of their income. Today that figure has changed to less than one percent while the rest of the world is still saving. This is the main reason America has turned to foreign investors. The Chinese for instance are said to save an average of 25 percent of their incomes. Simply put, Americans just aren't saving.

So what is the difference between Americans and the rest of the world that gives us these impulses to spend rather than save? A big part of it is globalization. In 2005 then Fed governor (now Chairman) Ben Bernanke told us that we were doing the world a favor by borrowing its surplus savings. Americans counted on overseas savers to lend them money, said Bernanke, and the overseas savers counted even more on Americans to go on spending splurges requiring that they borrow the money.

The biggest gap in Mr. Bernanke's analysis is the most essential part: the borrower must eventually pay back the lender. The lender becomes disappointed if the borrower cannot pay them back. This is a problem for Americans because the average income has become stagnant and is actually falling. With globalization came more better equipped and organized competition than in any other time since the beginning of the industrial revolution. People around the world are willing to work for pennies on the dollar. In light of this competition why would wages in the U.S. go up? If wages don't go up how can Americans pay back their enormous debts? With almost no savings and high spending it is nearly impossible.

The problem with our society is that we have everything. It has been that way for a long time. The dollar has been so strong for so long that people take it for granted. Every other nation in the world has wanted to do business with America for that very reason for a long time. The world accepts our currency as though it is real money with real value. A $100 bill looks like gold to many foreigners. You can buy a shipment of overseas electronics for a wad of $100 bills. And what is even more phenomenal is that they use the bills to buy another form of U.S. paper, Treasury bonds. We consume like no other society in the world because of this perception of our grand society and unfailing dollar. This is the most negligent thing that Americans could do.

Let's take a look at where America is in regards to our debt situation. As of September 2006 our outstanding public debt is almost 8.5 trillion dollars. The national debt has continued to rise an average of $1.54 billion per day since September 30, 2005. The sad thing is that there is no effective plan to resolve it.

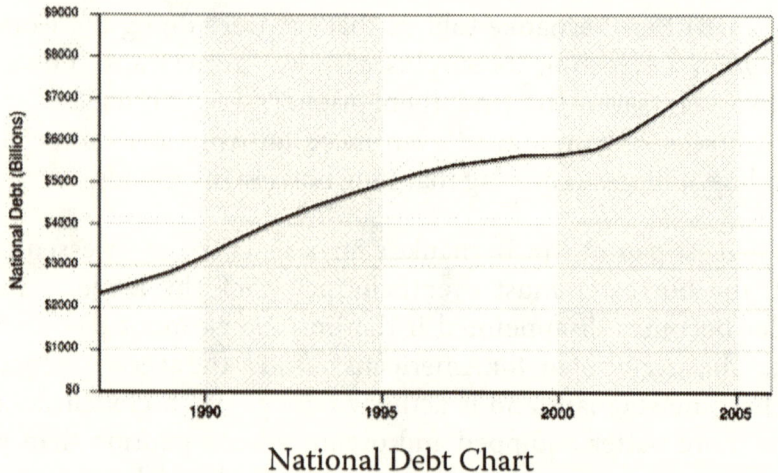

National Debt Chart

In a letter written by Thomas Jefferson to James Madison, Jefferson asked if "one generation of men has a right to bind another." The response to his own question was a loud "NO!" He went on to say, "No generation can contract debts greater than may be paid during the course of its own existence."

Think about it in this way. Say a man buys a house and establishes a mortgage. During the course of repaying the mortgage he falls over dead with a heart attack. In his will he leaves the house to his children, with the mortgage still outstanding. The children have no obligation to take the house because they are not involved in the mortgage contract. They can simply turn it down and let it go back to the bank if it is too burdensome. The same thing could be said with any debt that the man has left. The children are not expected to pay for it if they were not party to the contract.

Public debt on the other hand is a different thing. This is how it works: one generation consumes and runs the debt up and leaves the next generation to pay it down. However, the younger generation never agrees to the debt. So instead of paying the debt off by saving, the next generation does the same as the first, and so goes the never-ending debt cycle. The previous generation has no worries because after all, dead men don't worry.

Of course the politicians caught on to this very early. The way our system is set up there is no pressure put on the government to pay down the debt and so each new generation succumbs to the same temptations as the previous. They get the benefits of spending money right now while passing the debt onto the next generation or group of politicians that take over.

War has always been a reason for excess spending. During every war throughout American history, and world history for that matter, large debts have been amassed. Up until World War I the debts that had accumulated had always been paid down or paid off completely.

During World War I federal debt rose from $3 billion to over $26 billion. Then during the administrations of Harding and Hoover it was paid down to $16 billion. This was still far more than any other debt that had been accumulated up until this point in American History. But then the Great Depression took the nation by storm, along with President Roosevelt, and World War II. By 1945, federal debt had reached a staggering $260 billion. Just when it should have been over and the debts paid back another war started. It was the beginning of the Cold War and the debts continued to increase.

Over the next thirty years or so, the federal debt continued to soar. Several military skirmishes and the Vietnam War took place during this era. By 1980 the federal debt was over one trillion dollars. By the time Ronald Reagan left office in 1988 the debt headed for the moon once again reaching over 2.7 trillion dollars.

Then the Gulf war came and by the time George W. Bush took office, the debt had risen to $5.7 trillion. At this time hopes were high that our federal debt would start to get paid down. Peace was in the air and President Bush, a conservative, looked like the man to get the job done. Then the unthinkable happened: 9/11. Now instead of a war that could be measured by the taking of ground we were fighting an enemy that was not on any particular map. This began the War on Terror. The following 24 months after 9/11 America accrued more debt than had been accumulated in the first 200 years of existence.

You would think this would be a time when the government and the Fed would urge Americans to revert back to savings instead of spending borrowed money. But you see it is convenient for the public as well as the government to avoid the mess that we are in at all costs. After all we can just pass the buck on to the next generation like our forefathers did. But then again there may not be time.

We should be concerned about the exploding debt situation. So who are the debt culprits and what makes up this scary machine of debt? The answer is threefold: the Federal Government, the Financial Sector, and the Household Sector.

As of the fiscal year ending on September 30, 2005, the federal government's debt rose to over $7.9 trillion. If we divide the fiscal year 2005 ending debt of $7.933 by the total population of 296.5 million we have the debt per person at $26,750. This translates into $107,000 in federal debt responsibility for a family of four, including those not able to talk.

Estimated National Debt
$8,792,511,877,373.97

Share of National Debt for Each U.S. Citizen	$29,201.60
Share of National Debt for a Family of 2	$58,403.21
Share of National Debt for a Family of 3	$87,604.81
Share of National Debt for a Family of 4	$116,806.42
Share of National Debt for a Family of 5	$146,008.02
Share of National Debt for a Family of 6	$175,209.63

Total National Debt and Household
Portion Based on Size of Family

Our nation's founders were vehemently opposed to federal debt. After the American Revolution our leaders were concerned about the debts incurred to finance the war. At the writing of the constitution they vowed to promptly pay it off. Alexander Hamilton called for the "extinguishment of all debt." Thomas Jefferson later wrote, "I place economy among the first and most important of republican virtues, and public debt as the greatest of dangers to be feared." It sounds like debt should be placed as public enemy number one.

Is the debt going down? Not even by a penny! In 2005 federal debt was $554 billion more than the prior year. During the period since the September 11, 2001 terrorist attack on the World Trade Center, federal government debt increased by $2.1 trillion. Some ask, "Shouldn't it be okay to incur more debt since we are fighting a war?" Well let me ask this: Has our government reduced non-defense spending to fund our protection? The answer is no, it actually increased. I am not trying to make our government look bad, but they have to have some accountability. If we don't stand up for what is right this enormous debt will get passed on to our children and their children and they will suffer.

How Did We Get Here???

The repeating pattern of other ancient and modern civilizations gives us a clear picture of where the U.S. is headed. Every one falls in like manner, expanding government to address the people's perceived needs, accumulating too much debt, and then denying its financial obligations by destroying its own currency. So if the U.S. is to follow this pattern, there are three things that should be taking place. One, the government should be increasing in size; two we should be borrowing more and more money; and three we should be supporting this debt load by creating an ever larger amount of fiat currency. Unfortunately if we were to ask if the U.S. is following in these footsteps the answer would be a resounding yes.

The first problem in the equation is the growth of the government. The founders of our nation intended for the government to be limited to handling key functions like national defense, ensuring fair play between the states, and protecting private property and other rights by preserving the rule of law. At the beginning this remained the foundation, but as the founders grew older and died off so did their ideas. The first signs of change took place during the civil war. The focus in Washington was turned to control over banking and money.

Of course wars are always pressing needs and we have had our fair share of wars. Following World War I and during the misery of the Great Depression the government spawned new welfare programs, like Social Security, and a centralized bank regulatory regime. Amazingly enough, from 1930 to 1940, federal spending as a share of gross domestic product doubled from 4 to 8 percent.

With the poverty of the 1960s came "Great Society" programs like Medicaid, Medicare, and food stamps. The animal had been created. In 1950, welfare spending was roughly 12 percent of the federal budget. Today it consumes over 40 percent. By 1990 Medicare was about ten times more expensive than originally forecast.

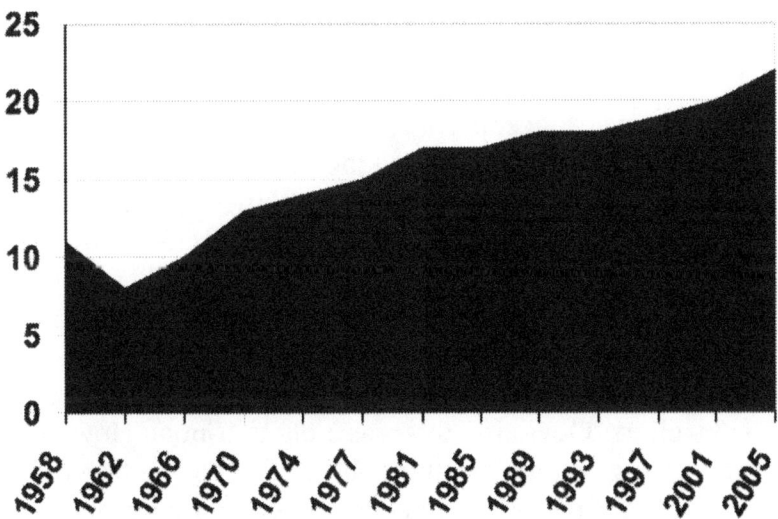

U.S. GOVERNMENT EMPLOYEES
FEDERAL, STATE, LOCAL
1958-2005

Source: U.S. Bureau of Labor Statistics
U.S. Government Employees

The steepness of the government's growth is astounding. In the 1920s the federal government took only 5 percent of the national income; today that figure has increased to nearly 25 percent. During Washington's time in office he spent only $20 per US citizen; in 2003 it was a staggering $7800. In 1946, there were 2.3 state and local government employees for every 100 citizens. Today there are 6.5. More Americans now work for the government than work in manufacturing.

The Debt Machine

Unfortunately what all of this means is that debts are soaring. Every time the government expands, lawmakers are faced with a dilemma: Do we raise taxes, cut spending or borrow and debauch the currency? And so the choice is easily made to spend more, save less, and borrow to keep tax hikes to a minimum. As a result the government's debts are steadily increasing.

So what do we do at this point? Spend, spend, and spend. Yet another war (a valid one), the war on terror has allowed Washington to turn the Debt Machine on full blast.

But here is an even bigger problem: all of this government spending and debt that we have been talking about up until this point does not even include the unfunded liabilities of Social Security and Medicare. Until recently the figures for these payouts were thought to be around 4 trillion dollars; however these numbers were wrong. In 2003 the treasury department reran the numbers according to the stricter standards that apply to the private sector and found out that the unfunded liabilities weren't $4 trillion, but $43 trillion. Obviously this was a big boo-boo. How did the numbers change so drastically? This is due to the fact that we are getting older faster. At present there are 4 current workers supporting every Social Security and Medicare recipient. But as the birthrates fall and populations age, in just a short period there will be only two workers to support each U.S. retiree. Add that statistic to the soaring cost of medical care and you have a soaring problem. These massive costs are not adequately funded and the government knows it. So eventually because of the pressure to fix the problem they will expand and grow even more.

It's Not Only Uncle Sam!

Household debt is another reflection of how the moods of the citizens are. The 1990s saw an increase in plastic surgery, luxury homes and gas-guzzling SUVs. On the other hand when the economy slows down and investments aren't doing so hot we tend to be more reserved in our spending habits. During these times we tend to pay off debt rather than indulge ourselves in the luxuries of life. Institutions are usually the same way. They tend to tighten their lending requirements and cut off the less credit-worthy customers. This usually results in the decline of the amount of debt an individual American carries.

This was not the mood, however, during our last recession. After the tech-stock crash, 9/11 and the war on terror in Iraq and Afghanistan you would think Americans would be pinching every penny and saving every dollar. Instead we turned it on full tilt and borrowed more than at any other time in history. And to make it possible the lenders made it easy for less creditworthy customers to get credit and the Fed lowered the rates to 1 percent. You've seen the ads "Bad Credit, No Credit, No Problem." This is absolutely absurd.

And of course if you receive mail then you know exactly what the credit card companies have been doing. Just about every day there is a new offer coming in for a pre-approved credit card. Then there is the auto industry dropping interest rates to zero percent, making it possible for people to take on debt with out any out-of-pocket obligation.

Oh, but that isn't the worst of it! We can't leave out the biggest of them all: the mortgage boom. In 2000 instead of home values falling, like the tech stocks in which many people were so heavily invested, they continued to rise. Consumers quickly caught on to this and started cashing out to maintain the lifestyle they had once so richly enjoyed. Of course it was all made possible by the lower interest rates. Banks like Wells Fargo and Bank of America began promoting their home equity lines of credit like never before. In 1997 mortgage borrowing averaged around $220 million annually, but in 2003 it soared to over $700 billion.

So why exactly would all of these smart bankers make it so easy for people with less-than-perfect credit to finance so much debt? Greed is definitely one factor. The more they lend the more their companies make, which in turn makes Wall Street investors happy because of the soaring stock prices. Then of course the top executives get their fat retirement package and they don't have to worry about the consequences of their actions. But greed isn't the only reason and neither is it the most important. The fact that the money that is lent is no longer the bank's money makes it all possible. It is called Securitization.

In the old days of banking when a banker gave you a loan they were planning on holding the note until the loan was paid off. Each loan was different which made it hard for outside investors to analyze how much this bag of credit was worth. So they stayed away from it. This of course made the banks choose their clients wisely because they would have to hold onto the paper until it was paid for.

Then in the 1980s the light kicked on for a few Wall Street gurus who figured out that if you bundled small, dissimilar loans together and turned them into high-grade bonds that investors would flock to the trough. So now hundreds of millions of dollars are being packaged and sold in a global market the world over every year. Now lenders don't have to be concerned with the creditworthiness of a borrower since they do not have to deal with the consequences of their mistakes. Rather the people who buy the bonds are the ones who will suffer. So now the lender is happy because his stock goes up, the investor is happy for the meantime, and household debt in the U.S. soars. To be more exact, since 1995 housing debt has more than doubled and is now over $7 trillion. I believe that what we have seen is a housing bubble bigger than any other in U.S. history, which will eventually make the bursting of that bubble bigger than any other in U.S. history. We will talk more about this in a later chapter.

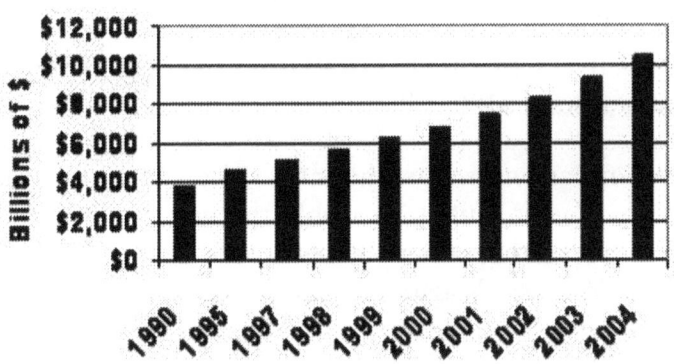

U.S. Housing Debt
1990-2004

Source : Federal Reserve

Total U.S. Housing Debt

What About Businesses?

Consumers aren't the only ones to take advantage of the low interest rates in recent years. Businesses have amassed their fair share of debt also. As interest rates have moved to the lowest point in recent history, businesses have been issuing bonds and commercial paper as fast as they can draw up the paperwork. Between 1995 and 2001 non-financial U.S. companies took on a total of $3.5 trillion in new liabilities. Since then these companies have added another $2.5 trillion of debt.

But here is a word that is even scarier than debt for these companies: derivatives. A derivative is a contract or security that derives its value from that of an underlying asset (as another security) or from the value of a rate (as of interest or currency exchange) or index of asset value (as a stock index). That is about the shortest definition I can give. I could literally write an entire book on derivatives but I won't. Derivatives can range anywhere from stock options to things that only the brightest of mathematicians can understand. A derivative basically works by dividing the risk associated with an underlying asset into pieces, allowing them to be sold to different people. Just like securitized debt, derivatives are being used at un-proportionate levels. Since 1994, the notional value (i.e. the dollar amount of the underlying financial instruments) of U.S. derivatives exposure has risen from an already enormous $10 trillion to around $100 trillion.

This presents an enormous amount of risk given the huge numbers involved. Warren Buffet, probably the greatest investor of our time, when speaking of derivatives not too long ago said they are "weapons of mass destruction" that pose a "mega-catastrophic risk."

The Big Picture

So let's take a look at the big picture. Right now as we have already seen, America's debt is not proportionately balanced and is soaring out of control. In the chart on the following page you will see the staggering difference between the per capita debt and the per capita GDP. The lower line represents the growth in GDP from 1960 to 2005. GDP is our total national income, or to simplify, it is what you get when you add up all the paychecks and sales receipts for a given year.

U.S. PER CAPITA DEBT AND GDP

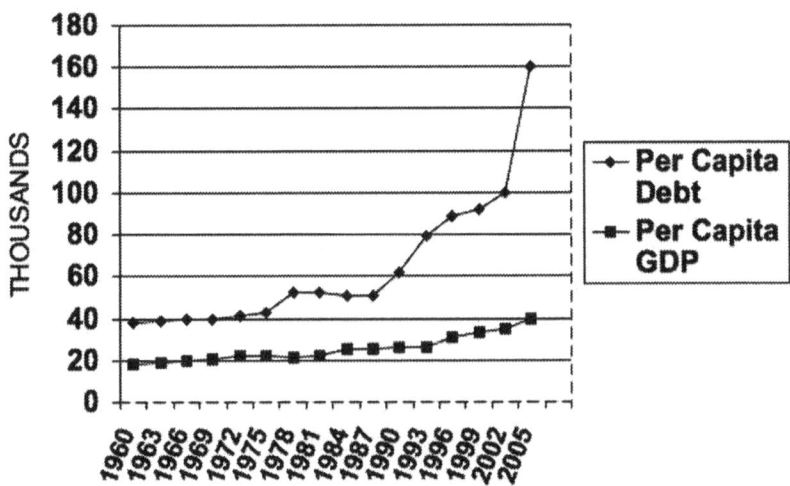

Source: Federal Reserve
U.S. per capita debt and GDP

The other line is the total debt that U.S. government, households and businesses have accumulated. Up until the middle of the 1980s the two lines track fairly closely. This simply implies that our borrowing was producing an equal amount of wealth up until about 1985. However, after 1985 the lines diverge, with the GDP continuing its steady growth while the debt growth soared. In the 1980s our debt increased by $9.5 trillion while GDP grew by $2.4 trillion. So if I am doing the math correctly that means we borrowed three dollars for every dollar of new income that we generated. In the 1990s it became even more serious with the debt increasing by $15 trillion while the GDP stayed steady at about $3 trillion. It basically went from a 3-1 ratio to a 5-1 ratio.

In total we currently owe about $43 trillion. That's more than 3 times the GDP and comes to about $155,000 per U.S. citizen. So if you have a family of four your portion of the debt is about $620,000. These numbers don't even take into account the $43 trillion dollars in unfunded trust-fund liabilities, and U.S. corporations' $100 trillion in derivatives exposure. Do you remember the three

23

requirements of a currency crisis? Well as you can see the U.S. has already met two of those requirements: Government spending and expansion and debt are on a rocket ship up.

CHAPTER 3

Trade Imbalance

I hear analysts and other financial people say, "We have sustained this amount of debt for a long time, who is to say we cannot continue to function like this forever?" The only problem with that theory is that we are not the only ones who have a say in the value of the dollar. Foreign investors who hold about 46% of our debt have a very big say, and in the next few years they may move in a very negative direction.

The U.S. is a major trading nation exporting everything from computers, to software, to food, and many other things. The same goes for imports except that the list gets a lot longer. The difference between what we buy and what we sell is known as either a surplus or a deficit. In a deficit environment we make up the difference by shipping dollars overseas. In the recent past we have been buying a considerable amount more than we have been selling. Thus we have a very large trade deficit. From the 1980s to the 1990s the trade deficit increased by over $220 billion. In 2003 it was over $500 billion and at the end of 2005 it was at an all-time high of $804.9 billion. This is well over 5% of the GDP, and countries who have reached this level in the past have not been able to sustain the value of their currency.

So if buying and selling are the two main ingredients in our trade imbalance, why don't we sell more and buy less? One very strong reason is that our companies can make basic products a lot cheaper in places like China, where intelligent and hard working people about earn about 1/10 of the prevailing U.S. wage. So for short-term bottom line growth it makes sense for companies to shut down their factories here and build them there. Wal-Mart is seen as one of the biggest players and driving forces behind this new move. Although this may seem good to the consumer right now as the savings are passed on to them, in the long run it will only hurt the economy. Why? It is very simple. When companies like Wal-Mart buy from foreign factories at cheaper prices and pass the savings on to consumers, it forces other companies to do one of two things: shut down or make the same move in order to compete. As a result foreign factories are flooding the U.S. market with cheap goods that used to be made right here in the good ol' U S of A. This has thrown our trade balance with China way out of proportion while just a few years ago we were pretty evenly balanced. Currently we run a $200 billion per year deficit with China alone.

If it were just China that would be just dandy and it would definitely be manageable. But unfortunately it isn't just China. We are currently running trade deficits with Japan and the EU of over $80 billion and $120 billion respectively. Then of course there is the situation of oil imports (to be discussed in a later chapter in more detail), which seem to be heading nowhere but up. The most reasonable conclusion is that most Americans are addicted to a lifestyle that cannot be supported. We need bigger houses, bigger cars and better toys than ever before. The sad part is we are willing to go to any expense of borrowing to get it. This is an unsustainable lifestyle.

Don't let the media fool you. When looked at truthfully our trade situation is unprecedented. We run an annual trade deficit larger than both the budgets of Social Security and the military. Our manufacturing base has declined from 30% of GDP in 1959 to less than 10% today.

So what are these other nations doing with all of those dollars? They have been piling them up. Their central banks have been doing this in order to support their own currencies, while at the same time foreign businesses have been buying real estate, bonds, stocks and other U.S. investments. Foreign investors now own a considerable amount more of our investments than we do of theirs. The current amount of U.S. assets held by foreign investors exceeds $9 trillion, including "13% of all stocks, 13% of agencies, and 27% of corporate bonds", according to Gillespie Research/Federal Reserve. The major provider of money for home mortgages is Fannie Mae—guess where they get that money? They borrow about a third from outside the U.S., according to *Bloomberg Report* (*Bloomberg Report*, September 2002).

Additionally, foreign interests own real estate and factories. During the 1980s, the U.S. was the world's largest creditor nation, which means we had a whole lot more invested in other nations compared to what they had invested in us. Now the tables have turned and we are the world's largest debtor nation.

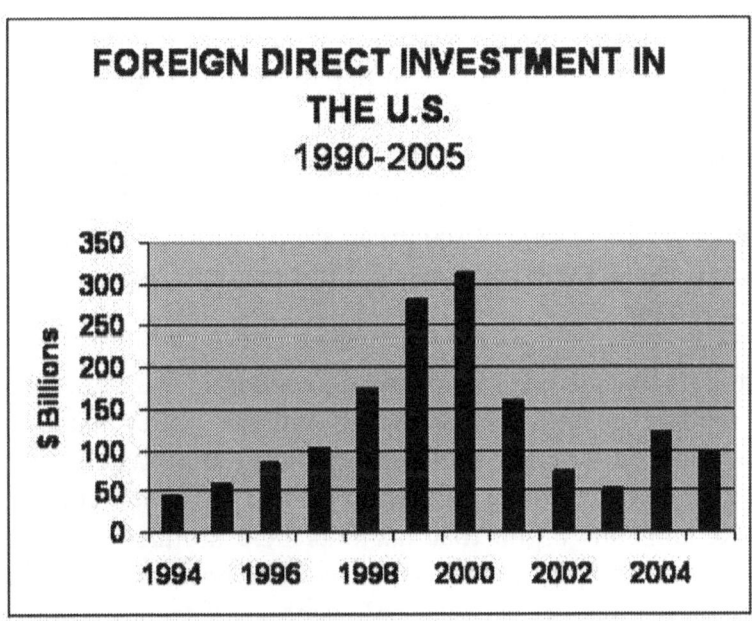

Source: Federal Reserve
Foreign Direct Investment

The Catch-22 is this. As long as these foreign countries remain willing to pump their dollars back into the U.S. economy we will remain stable. But if, and really when, they change their mind and decide not to buy U.S. assets we are in for some serious trouble. This is one of the main reasons why Warren Buffet has been holding over 20 billion dollars in euros since 2003. Since 2000 foreign direct investment has been on a steady decline, falling from $300 billion to less than $100 billion. Not to mention the struggle that the dollar has been through in recent years. In 2003 we saw a sharp decline versus the euro and the yen. However even though foreign investors recycled fewer dollars back into our economy they continued to buy our assets. In 2005 they bought over $99 billion in foreign assets. So now their stake in the U.S. continues to rise, but the moment they begin to sell their stake in our stocks, bonds and real estate the debt problem will become very real. What exactly will happen? Well in theory the dollar will weaken even further, which will set off a chain reaction of foreign investors looking elsewhere for investment opportunity. This in turn will cause the demand for dollars to go into a serious drought. Needless to say we are treading some very deep waters.

Many people in our government believe that deficit spending is a positive force, working to improve the economy, while at the same time having no negative effect. Congress seems to agree with this point of view seeing that they continue to spend greater amounts of public money. One of the greatest oppositions to any type of reform is the fact that congress does not seem to see public money as real money.

Adding to this already complicated problem is the class warfare surrounding government spending and tax policy itself. The Democrats' outlook of course is to criticize "huge tax cuts for the rich" while putting more of a strain on less fortunate Americans. The Republicans argue that tax cuts help stimulate economic growth and add jobs to the economy. The bottom line is that it really doesn't matter if we raise or lower taxes if spending outpaces revenue. Of course the higher taxes will have a direct impact on consumers while higher government spending that continues to outpace its own revenues does more damage in the long run.

There is a very important difference between government deficits and personal deficits. To many these differences are quite obvious, but I would like you to read one report given by Congress that did a good job of comparing the two. This report statement simply points out that an individual is able to offset debt by reducing spending and working harder. The report notes:

> *In contrast, government revenue comes mainly from taxes, which are compulsory. When government increases its revenue by increasing tax collections, there is no presumption that people will be better off. They may not want to give more of their income to the government. Therefore, closing a budget deficit by raising more revenue does not necessarily make our economy grow; it can discourage growth by making leisure time and other untaxed activity relatively more attractive. Raising tax rates, or keeping them higher than they need to be, increases what economists call the "deadweight loss" or "excess burden" of taxation-income that is not transferred from taxpayers to government, but is simply lost because excessive taxation reduces economic growth by inducing people to behave less productively. (Joint Economic Committee, United States Congress: "Deficits, Taxation, and Spending," April 2003; and "Hidden Cost of Government Spending," staff report, 2001)*

Although this observation is true, it only deals with part of the problem. If you look back at history it is plain to see that tax policy does not help to eliminate deficits. Increased taxes have never and will never close budget deficits or trade deficits. Raising taxes has influenced Congress to spend ever-increasing amounts of money. Reducing taxes has always had one of the two following outcomes: either lower taxes only add to the deficit, or the resulting "trickle down" revenues result in higher spending, which leads to higher deficits.

So we are still left with the argument that deficit spending helps the economy through stimulus. Actually, the government believes that the role it plays is a driving force that can and should take steps to fix recessions or curb inflation. During recession, the proposal to increase government spending is invariably argued as a strategy for remedying the problem. (Joint Economic Committee: "Deficits, Taxation, and Spending.")

This argument is not rational. Let me ask you: What does the government produce? The answer: Nothing. So there is no logical way that increased spending would have a positive effect on the economy. If the argument were made in the light of increasing investment in manufacturing plant and equipment, providing incentives for higher savings, or actually reducing government deficit spending, it might make sense. But claiming that higher spending on the part of the government would fix an economic recession is like claiming that making a wound deeper is going to stop the bleeding.

There are few situations where deficit spending has a positive impact on the economy. These situations are very limited and few and far between. When such spending is used to relocate resources from less productive use and into more productive use, it is conceivable that deficit spending would improve the economy. But most of the time government spending has the opposite effect of relocating resources from more productive use and into less productive use.

The fact that tax policy has historically been ineffective in its attempt to control the economy could be in whole or in part due to the fact that tax policy has been used to either reward or punish. Tax policy has contributed more to the widening gap between classes than any other single force in U.S. history. Government simply cannot control the thermostat of the economy using tax policy.

Domestic monetary policy has its foundation in various causes, including current account deficit, increased borrowing and spending, loss of competitive edge, and the removal of the U.S. dollar from the gold standard. After 1971, when Nixon took the dollar off of the gold standard, a major shift happened in the growth of the trade balance. Within 5 years of that decision, the trade surplus turned into a trade deficit. After about ten years following the shift the current account balance followed sharply downward as well.

What does this mean in regards to the dollar? It means that the dollar has lost a significant amount of purchasing power. As the dominant power in the manufacturing market of the world the U.S. dollar has always been king. But all of that has begun to change now that the dollar has given up that lead. As a result the dollar has fallen against other major world currencies. The European currency is one of the main beneficiaries.

The strength of the euro over the past few years is a direct result in the shifts in international trade and manufacturing and in the outlook on future investment rates of return. Most U.S. economists agree amongst themselves that Europe's economy is mainly export driven, however this has been proven to be wrong. The falling U.S. dollar has not hurt European exporting by creating cheaper imports in the United States. The fact that American consumers have a very large hunger for goods has held import prices up.

Prolonged weak productivity from the U.S. and record low interest rates are beginning to make America extremely unattractive to foreign investors. The results of this will be an even sharper decline in the U.S. dollar.

Because of the United States failure to stop the trade gap from worsening in the late 1970s we are in a deeper hole with more severe consequences. Once the surplus vanished and deficits began to increase we should have taken immediate action to remedy the problem. But no one at that time understood the consequences of those decisions and certainly no one understood the impact it would have on the dollar's long-term purchasing power. The euro's rise to the dollar is not necessarily based on economic changes from Europe. Rather the rise in the euro against the dollar is based upon adverse economic and financial trends. These trends are doing serious damage to the value of the dollar versus other currencies. As the dollar falls the value of the other currencies rise.

The current account deficit is the major underlying factor in the value changes between the currencies. There are various changes that I see need to be made to fix the problem. They include adjustments in the exchange rates; a slowdown in U.S. growth, more specifically in consumer spending; and improvement in foreign demand for U.S. goods. Additionally as these changes are made there needs to be a dramatic reduction in the trade deficit.

The adjustments can only be brought about by changes in domestic policy, or else worldwide economic changes will force the adjustment. One major concern among policy makers is the difference in exchange rates, not necessarily the fact that as one currency rises another falls, but more because of the structure of U.S. assets versus U.S. debts. Nearly half of U.S. foreign assets are denominated in foreign currencies, but the vast majority of our liabilities are dollar denominated. This difference in currencies could have unintended consequences based on the movement in the currency values of the dollar as well as other currencies.

Oftentimes U.S. policymakers will force changes in the restrictive policies. Many times this does not work, as seen when President Nixon took the dollar off the gold standard and imposed a trade surcharge in domestic wage price controls. History shows us that naturally that did not work. Today we face a similar challenge in fixing the current account deficit. It is highly unlikely that any trade restrictions will help resolve this problem. The more likely solution will come by exchange rate adjustments, a drastic slowing of U.S. consumer demand, and a trend toward increased demand in other countries.

The dollar, which has been our ace in the hole so to speak, is the card that holds everything else hanging in the balance.

The U.S. stock market and the demand for goods and products overseas are going to be the key to the U.S. dollar's strength. Unfortunately changes in both of these are outside of the control of the day. As Alan Greenspan discovered in 2004, you can only lower interest rates so much. It's going to take much more to continue to finance our current day. It's going to require a new financial bubble. Of course this bubble will not last forever either. Although chances of a new bull run in the stock market are very slim, it could happen. Eventually our bluffs are going to be called. When that happens it will be too late to create real solutions.

In recent years we have seen the dollar top, fall down and continue to fall against the euro. After all, the dollar's strength has been borrowed. What this means for us is that our purchasing power will continue to slide and as a result the trade deficit will get worse and the dollar will further weaken. This is what happened in the years 1985 through 1987 when the deficit rose very quickly even though the dollar's value virtually collapsed. The fed has set in motion policies that are both unrealistic and damaging.

The problems we're facing in the days ahead are appearing real and very serious. I once heard that it takes a locomotive 70 miles to slow down after reaching full speed; this, of course, is without the use of brakes. It is called momentum. Momentum can be good or it can be bad. The United States has reached full speed in its debt and deficit disorder. Some of the problems we face are recapped in the next sentences.

1) Reduced foreign investment. A slowing down among foreign lenders is a sign that we are reaching our credit capacity. Once investors are worried about getting repaid they immediately begin cutting off the credit supply.

2) Continuing slow demand for U.S. goods. The slow pace of demand for U.S. goods is often cited as the cause of the trade

deficit. It is a painful symptom of the port competitiveness of the United States. If we are to fix that problem we must aggressively attack it by revising international pricing which is a difficult task.

3) Unfavorable currency exchange rates. Unfortunately credit-based spending is hurting our dollar. As this continues the attrition rate of the dollar will continue also. This affects our purchasing power not only for the consumer at the mall or on vacation in Europe, but also for U.S. business capital investment.

In opposition to these theories, some contrarians believe that there will be a fierce rally of the dollar. In fact we have seen quite a rally in the recent past. However this rally does not change the looming facts of our deficit disorder.

We have to look at the total picture of the problem, not just that one rally. What about the trading current account deficit flattening the factory record, growing consumer debt, and so on? The harsh reality is these problems must be fixed before we can see a true change in where our dollar is heading. Sometimes an individual can have on a personal level and get out of the tight squeeze; this does not often work in economic situations. The rabbit does not simply pop out of the hat when it comes to looming deficits and large debts.

We must set a new trend in motion if we expect the dollar to change direction. If we continue on the same path we will have the same results. Our risk is the unprecedented levels in the history of our nation. The risk is far higher than similar adjustments that were needed in the past. Today, the risk that the dollar will fall is inevitable. It is not just based on pie in the sky theory; it is based on our exposure to risk in the trillions of dollars of foreign holdings in U.S. dollars. The exchange risk involved in this is significant. That change in the transitional dollar in a weak euro is highly unlikely, however the trend of the rising euro against a falling dollar is much more likely.

CHAPTER 4

Stock Market Blues

The nineties were a crazy time. Most retirees were walking around with huge smiles on their faces. Some of them even had taken on new careers as day traders. Most of them were buying stocks based on hunches, rumors, recent headlines, etc. There were no in-depth studies or analyses of the markets taking place in most of these cases, nor were these men or women even seeing if they were beating the stock market in general. What did get their attention was that their net worth, on paper, was increasing daily. Most of them believed they had discovered a fountain of gold.

The strange thing was that most of American society believed the same thing. It was the techno revolution and profits were high across the board. Computer nerds, most of whom were not seen as giants in the business world, were given hundreds of millions of dollars to pursue their latest technology ventures. The idea was that their dot-com companies did not have to make a profit; rather the idea was to develop a customer base using information technology, and the profits would follow. Most of them formulated their success from the number of visitors they had to their web sites. They didn't bother estimating how much profit or even a way that they would make a profit. The idea was to generate customers and profits would come later. Venture capitalists and investors believed them.

Not only was the private investor sucked in to this dangerous trap, CEOs of large companies who should have known better looked at these dot-com companies in awe. Most of these executives were techie wannabes who tried to make their companies look like dot-com companies. Almost all of them took crash courses on how to use the 'Net. One CEO even bragged that investors looked at their company like a dot-com company. Any project having interaction with the 'Net got direct priority corporate funding. Many of the corporate heads of this day also did what was necessary to make their stocks look like dot-com stocks. The truth is that most of the financial gains of this era came from accounting creativity that made the corporate performance look stellar by pushing costs into future years and doing other financial wizardry.

Baby boomers were a big part of this new move in the stock market. What drove it was the desire for them to make the gains their parents made in the stock market. Many of them began buying up stocks as fast as they could. As more stocks were bought, demand was driven up while supply was limited, which in turn drove up the prices of the stocks. As a result of this buying pressure, the later years of the last century saw phenomenal gains in the stock market.

Anyone who was able to capitalize on the gains of the nineties in the stock market was fortunate indeed. If you would have bought S&P 500 stocks in 1994 and sold them in 1999, your investment would have tripled in value.

Unfortunately, that is not the way most people invest. Most people invest on a consistent basis and then hold their investment for a long period of time. This is also the savings method advised by most market experts. For example if someone invested a fixed amount every year, starting in 1994, and was still investing this fixed amount for 2003, they would only be ahead 33%.

Others have come to similar conclusions on the stock market. John Bogle, founder of the very successful company The Vanguard Group, Inc. estimates that the average return for equity funds from 1984 through 2001, a time which includes the great stock market bubble of the nineties, was just slightly more than inflation! On top of the disappointing performance are the fees charged by mutual funds and the turning of stocks. Both of these add to the costs of doing business in the stock market.

Most people have reviewed the nineties as the time of great gains made in the stock market. They continue to look at the 200% gain the Khudyan realized by buying in 1994 and selling in 1999.

Between the years 1990 and 2000 due to the baby boomer surge the number of people in the age group 30 to 54 increased almost 25%. These are the primary stock buying interests. Below the age of 30, people are involved with getting an education or starting their careers. Once people become 55, some of them begin to move investments into more conservative areas, getting ready for retirement.

Along with the surge in potential stock buyers came an increasing awareness of and participation in the stock market. Stock ownership by families went from 23% to over 56% in the period 1990 to 2001. This increased stock market interest, along with the previously noted increase of people aged 30 to 54, meant that there were approximately three times as many potential stock buyers at the end of last century that the beginning of 1990. Of course there are other explanations given for the nineties stock market craze but I see this as being the most simple.

Increased demand plays an important role in the price of stock. A relatively small percentage of stocks are in play on any given day. When one of these stocks becomes available for sale and there are very large numbers of people interested in buying the stock, the stock will trade at a higher price than normal due to the demand. This is an easy explanation for what happened in the nineties. As explained before there was not an in-depth analysis of stock prices and company values going on, there were just a lot of people who wanted to buy stocks because they believed stock prices were going higher.

This was not only seen with the individual investor, it was also seen with the professional picking stocks for the mutual funds. 401(k) savings plans generated an automatic increase in investment dollars that was eventually dumped on mutual fund managers' desks. The fund managers could only delay the investment of this money for a short period of time and would eventually have to pump it into the stock market. This in turn drove up the demand for the stocks.

Media coverage was also another driving force in the increase of the stock market. This caused many people to want to actively trade stocks on the Internet. The web helped fuel the fire of these new day traders and self-proclaimed experts. It also caused the cost of training to fall dramatically. With the advent of online brokers and online trading, people could trade from their homes or from their offices any time of day.

It's not hard to see how greed blinded the minds of these investors. Many of them began to extrapolate their gains for the next twenty years and saw themselves as millionaires within a short period of time. Of course their newfound success gave them no reason to continue to save outside of the stock market.

You would think at some point these people would stop to wonder if the stocks they were buying were overpriced, or whether the companies really had growth potential, or the simple fact that there was not enough money in the world for every investor to become truly wealthy. It was beyond their comprehension to conceive that when they finally decided to sell their stock, there would be no one to buy the stock. Maybe if their timing was right they could be one of the lucky early sellers and do very well. But it would be like a domino effect. The sellers after them would do worse and worse as a chain reaction continued.

In the nineties there were reports that claimed the Dow would reach 36,000 or even 100,000. The rationale for the huge estimated values was of course based upon future earnings that would never be realized. So, these books talking like there were no more risks when investing in the stock market and other more traditionally conservative investments such as bonds were false. Of course the comeback is that the stock market always comes back. Historically that is true, however there is another factor involved. If investors are able to handle the down draws of the market then they will eventually make their money back right? Well if the markets do come back that would definitely be true. Of course, the books forget to mention that when the effects of inflation are included, it may take well over twenty years before the investments recover. Most people's investment window couldn't tolerate that. Of course this could have been a humorous subject, if it weren't for the fact that many people risked their lifetime savings on the unrealistic dream of getting rich with no effort.

What eventually happened is that people started losing money. In the year 2000 the Motley Fool began to lose money. In case you aren't familiar with it, www.fool.com it is a website developed by two brothers named David and Tom Gardner that have a cadre of resources for stock investors. From 1994 to March of 2003 the brothers also operated The Fool Portfolio, also dubbed the "Rule Breakers Portfolio". Up until 2000, when the portfolio began to lose money, it was celebrated for its dramatic gains. It was starting to become obvious that information technology in most cases just enabled more junk mail and junk information. People that needed more information already had more than they could handle.

Of course if we look back in retrospect at the stock market price bubble we can see that the gross domestic product for the period was unaffected. Due to the way GDP works, if the companies of the stock market bubble had seen superb performance we would have been able to tell by looking at the GDP. The value of these new companies would have changed the output of the country in a very considerable manner. Instead we just see the GDP continue on a pretty even trend.

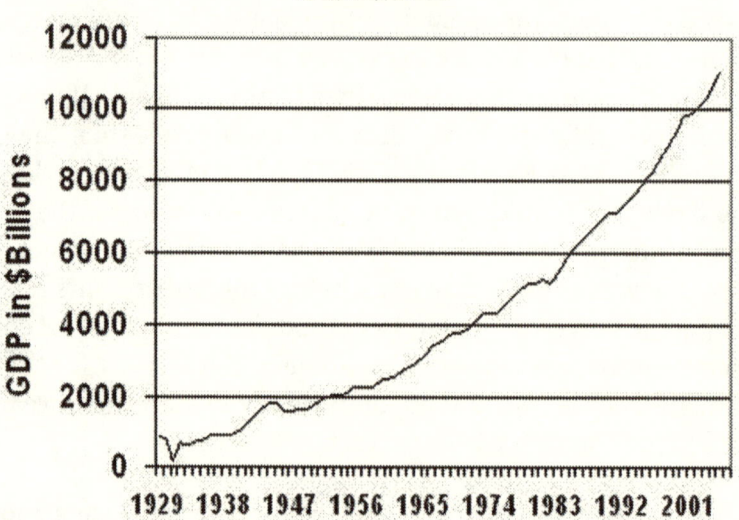

Source: Bureau of Economic Analysis

Real GDP Growth

The chart shows that in the nineties there were no sudden spikes or changes in the ongoing quantitative gain in the GDP. The line showing the GDP just continued upward at almost the same rate it had been for the past 45 years before the nineties. The information-driven society had absolutely no effect on the GDP.

Besides the GDP being off, if we take a look at the stock dividends we see the same thing. The stock dividends did not justify the high prices of stocks. Dividends are the criteria we must use to measure long-term company performance, because they are the profits the owners actually get out of their investments. If you bought a company, you might opt to use the initial earnings to grow the business or improve it. However at some point you are going to want to take some money out of the company for personal use. Dividend payouts can be delayed while growing a business;

but if the earnings never generate dividends then real earnings were either never there, were wasted on bad investments, or were used to enrich others pocketbooks rather than the owners of the business.

The fact that company earnings have proven to be easily manipulated in the recent past is evidence that it is hard to evaluate the rewards of a company using its earnings statements. The failures of Enron and the like are proof of the truth of this statement. In the nineties many companies became expert at making earnings up every year to be whatever they wanted. Real spending on research and development (R&D) was reduced in place by labeling all projects with even a small amount of risk as being the R&D. This indicator is misleading because it gives the appearance of future growth through continued investment, and at the same time the companies are able to capitalize on the immediate tax benefit. Individual pieces of equipment, which were previously depreciated separately, are bundled together and then amortized over a larger number of years. This reduces current expenses and makes profits look larger. It doesn't matter that it will be harder for them to replace individual pieces of equipment in the future as new technology makes them outdated, because to replace one piece the whole bundled assembly has to justify recapitalization. The previously expensed items are now classified as investments, making current earnings appear more robust by delaying current costs into the future while showing high investment numbers. Outsourcing generated immediate gains, but sacrificed the manpower skills needed to grow future business.

By looking at the GDP and dividends we can see that there was no real performance improvement that justified the dramatic rise in stock prices in the nineties. The most logical reason for the rising stock prices in the nineties is very simple. The unusually high demand for stocks, driven by the increase of the buyer base overwhelmed the supply of stocks. Of course there were some new dot-com companies added to the mix of stocks, but eventually these companies rewarded their investors by going bankrupt. The pressure on almost all the stocks to bid up to the high demand was intense. This is what I believe to be the main cause for the stock market rally in the nineties.

This series of events in the stock market of the nineties along with our debt situation encouraged large deficits, which started a series of events, which will lead to the next depression. One other reason why people stopped saving during the nineties was due to the highly inflated stock prices. They thought that the stock market gains would guarantee their future. On top of not saving most people took on large debt loads. Of course many of them didn't even know how they would pay the debts back. They just believed they would all become rich from their gains in the stock market.

CHAPTER 5

The Next "Great Depression"

Let me write a disclaimer before I begin this chapter. I want you to understand that I want our economy to succeed. So please do not write me letters telling me how big of a pessimist I am. I am an optimist to the core, however the facts don't lie. If I were an investor in the stock market I would want stock prices and the economy to do well. By the same token if I were an investor in real estate I would not want to accept that there could be a bursting of the housing bubble. But I am neither an investor in the stock market nor in real estate. So my point of view, which is simply a view from a point, is not emotionally attached. It's quite obvious that no one wants our country to sink into a severe depression. Unfortunately this positive outlook often times can blind people from seeing the reality. The harsh reality is that we have been living in excess for the past two decades. The price will have to be paid sooner or later.

What would you say if I described a place where there were more abandoned buildings than occupied ones? Or what if you saw a scene where elderly people were left to spend their last days in poverty because they had nothing left to show for their life but a remnant of broken promises of financial freedom given to them in their earlier years? Could you imagine living in a society with a shortage of hospital beds and medical care, or whole families who once were considered wealthy, now ruined? What if you were to drive through entire areas that were deemed lawless zones where the cops didn't even dare go?

The first thought that probably comes to your mind as I describe this scene is probably a third-world nation or a war-ravaged city like Baghdad. What if I told you that this could be America in the next five years or less? Most of you cannot fathom it, so you don't want to think about it. The truth is, as I have already laid out how civilizations fall, this could very well be America. We are not any more special or less susceptible than our foregoers.

I believe in the years ahead father will be set against son, mother against daughter, old versus young...locked in a material and ideological struggle far worse than anything we have ever seen in America.

I'm not describing another civil war where our nation destroys itself with weapons of mass destruction, but rather a more subtle war: A war in which no shots are fired, nonetheless a war that in the end may possibly leave America looking like a wasteland as money, wealth, and the American dream virtually vaporize overnight.

During the coming economic collapse income taxes will absolutely double and possibly even triple. Billions of dollars will disappear overnight from retirement accounts and pension funds. What about Social Security and Medicare? If you're lucky you may get back half of what you put in even if you are already at retirement age.

Oh, but that is just the beginning. The stock market will not only crash, it will collapse. Wall street will go on full tilt. Hospitals and schools will close doors. There will not be enough money to sustain our fire and police departments.

This is not something that has a slim possibility of happening; it absolutely will happen. Paul Volcker, former Fed Chairman and the economist who was phenomenal in Reagan's early days, says we have "a 75% chance of a major crisis over the next 5-10 years...." Steve Roach, the head honcho at Morgan Stanley, says he "can't imagine a more unstable disequilibrium."

This disaster probably won't happen tomorrow or next year, but it will happen. Most people cannot fathom the coming crisis; therefore they don't see the seriousness of it. Too many Americans are caught up in their own little bubble of comfort and can't imagine anything negative happening in their lifetime.

One thing is certain: when consumer spending dries up...and when stocks get dumped and factories close...when America makes the coming multibillion-dollar shift, the consequences will not be pretty.

Of course we have survived hardships and crisis in the past, so what is so different about this one? We have overcome the 9/11 attack on the heart of our financial empire. We survived the dot-com bust and the oil crisis of the 1970s and 80s. We've rebounded from costly wars.

But there has never been a nation in history that has been able to recover from as much debt as we are in. This debt peaks at over $76 trillion. As a matter of fact there has never been a nation in history with that kind of debt load.

And it's not only the debt. There are so many factors converging on us all at once. These looming crisis factors will create a financial collapse far worse than anything anybody living has ever seen. It will be worse than the economic depression our nation suffered in 1929.

It is a widely known fact that you cannot keep spending forever. This is true on an individual as well as a national level. If recent consumer spending were being fueled by an increase in consumer income then we would not be writing this chapter. But because individual debt has a maximum point, and because consumer debt spending and drawing down the savings rate close to zero has fueled the recent economy, there will be a slow down when the debt level reaches the maximum. I believe this is what will trigger the depression. As I am writing this book our economy has already begun to slow down. If we continue on this track a very large slowdown is inevitable.

As seen in the past, stocks can stay overpriced for many years. However overpriced stocks will not be the only catalyst to a downturn in the economy. If you remember in the mid-nineties some economists predicted an economic slowdown based on already really high stock prices. When the slowdown didn't happen they were given to the dogs. What will happen to the overpriced stocks in the downturn will be a severe correction. The market will fall to the point that the stocks are overpriced and then some.

In the coming depression I believe the people who are most likely be hurt are the middle class of society. Our country is already turning into a two-class society. There is an old saying that is ringing quite true among Americans: it is that the rich are getting richer and the poor are getting poorer. In the coming years the middle class society is going to go one way or the other. Some will get rich while others will get poor. During the Depression of the 1920s and in other nations that have seen economic depressions, we have seen that the people begin to act totally out of character. After all their economies are crashing down all around them. Their foundation is shaken. Everything that they have ever known is suddenly stripped away from them with very little they can do about it. Of course there are always those who are hurt more severely in a depression. That is why I believe it will be the middle class. They have the greatest to lose. After all it is not the rich people that have gone into severe debt over the past two decades. The poor haven't gone into debt because most poor people can't get credit. The middle class American is the culprit of the extreme debt shift over the past two decades. Therefore they will be the class most affected by this coming economic downturn.

Some of you are asking, well what about my pension and retirement funds, won't I still have those? Well maybe, or maybe not.

In 1996, General Motors spent $3 billion on health care for 1.2 million employees, retirees, and dependents. In 2004, it spent $5.2 billion on employees' healthcare. But we see it just keeps rising in 2005, with spending on healthcare for its employees reaching over $5.6 billion.

Now GM says it can't afford soaring health costs. It's in crisis. On top of that, the pensions that they are supposed to pay out are piling up too. They are in the same situation as the baby boomer consumer that is going to be relying on them. No savings, no cash, and feeling very desperate.

This is just one of many big companies that could go belly up in the future, leaving millions of employees with unpaid pension funds. Now I am not predicting that they will go belly up any time soon, but companies like this, including Ford and Chrysler, could be headed for some rocky roads. You see these big costs mixed with missed earnings have the potential to do serious damage to stock prices. And these giant corporations are exactly what are represented in pension funds and 401(k) plans across America.

So what happens when your company can't pay? Well the Pension Benefit Guaranty Corp. (PBGC) is supposed to help. However they already handle over 3,000 companies that can't cover their total pension bills.

Companies like Polaroid, TWA, SINGER, Bethlehem Steel, and many more rely on the PBGC. As if all this wasn't scary enough there's more. The PBGC, which was created to help save failing pension funds, is on the verge of failing itself. Right now the PBGC is currently in the red by $23.3 billion, with another $80 billion in private pension funds headed toward failure.

It is a tragedy waiting to happen, especially since companies that still offer pensions to employees are already under funded by as much as $350 billion!

You say, "Well I don't have a pension fund I have a 401(k). I'm safe right?" Wrong. The truth is that companies that have switched over to 401(k) plans have no insurance in place if the plans go into default. Meanwhile, in 2005 alone there were 1,269 cases in which companies didn't even deposit their employees designated payroll deductions into savings accounts. But the worst part about it is that out of 627,905 401(k) plans in the United States only 55,195 were even audited for fraud by the U.S. government.

But the big companies like GM have another looming problem. Take a look at the following chart and you will see why.

Who's Going to Do the Work?

Percentage of workers able to replace retiring "Boomers"

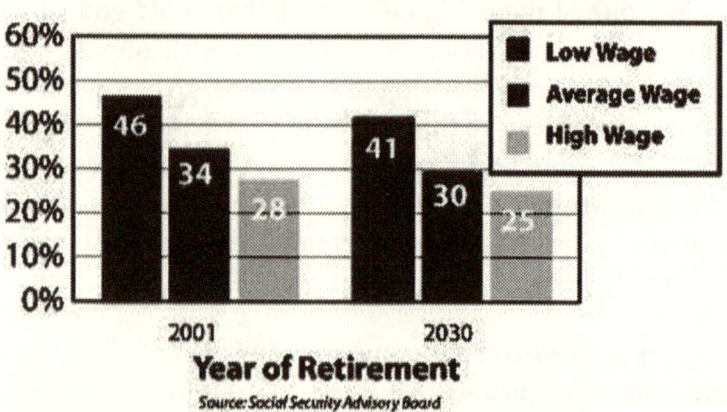

Year of Retirement

Source: Social Security Advisory Board

When Boomers start retiring in 2008, there won't be enough workers to fill their places. Productivity will fall. Companies will suffer. Stock prices will plunge.

In 2008 when boomers begin to retire by the millions, productivity across whole industries will begin to take a nosedive. Why? Simply because there will be far fewer younger workers coming onboard to take over their jobs. When productivity of these companies plunges the economy suffers, wages stay flat, and the stock market tanks.

That is bad news for your stock portfolio. You say "What if I am holding the investments in my portfolio for the long haul?" First of all, the buy and hold strategy doesn't always work. The reason I believe it has even less of a chance to work for the boomer generation is that it could take the market 30 or 40 years to recover after a period of great economic depression and it may never recover at all.

If you are 65 and looking at retiring soon do you have time to wait 30-40 years for the market to recover? The answer is definitely no. You will probably run through your funds long before you get ready to leave this planet.

The bottom line is that not everyone is going to get rich investing. As a matter if fact it is not possible for everyone to be rich. But it is possible for a whole lot of people to be poor, very poor.

The big problem with the boomer generation is that they have been depending on the stock market like it is some kind of printing press that is just going to print them as much money as they need when they need it. They pour money into their 401(k)s, bidding up each other's shares. My question to you is who is going to be left holding the bag now that the boomers are ready to pull out?

At today's mortality rates to retire with a $100,000 a year lifestyle, you need at least $1.5 million in savings. That number will shrink even quicker as inflation rises and the purchasing power of the dollar decreases as its value falls against other major world currencies.

As of last year only 50% of all workers between the ages of 25 and 65 have money in any other kind of investment besides Social Security. And half of all households aged 45-55, which is only 10 years away from retirement, have less than $46,000 in total net worth.

This includes insurance policies, bank accounts, and 401(k)s. Millions of Americans believe Social Security and Medicare will make up the shortfall. Unfortunately they couldn't be more wrong.

In a recent speech to the Economic Club of Washington, Ben Bernanke, the Federal Reserve Chairman, said the gradual aging of the population has major implications not only for federal programs for the elderly, such as Social Security and Medicare, but the broader economy.

These are the main reasons why I believe that sometime during 2007, American consumers will reach their maximum debt loads, which will cause the effects of the slowdown to begin to be felt in our economy. Consumer spending will only be part of the cause of the debt reaching its maximum limit. Outside forces such as the increased cost of living, which for the most part are now outside of the consumer's control, will rapidly hasten the economic slowdown. It will cause consumers to start reducing their spending, but it will be too late. The problem will arise when costs, such as energy, medical care and imported goods begin to rise so much that consumers cannot maintain their current debts. We have already seen gas prices increase over 60% across the board. Since 2001 the dollar has fallen 65% versus the euro. Also the Chinese have been toying with the idea of disassociating the value of their currency from the dollar, which will increase the cost of imported goods from China by more than 40%.

Another catalyst in the coming depression is the expensive wars in which the United States has recently been involved. Since 2001 when we experienced the worst terrorist attack in our history we have racked up the costs to protect our nation. We have implemented new "Homeland Security" policies, which have furthered the increase in these expenses. I believe these actions were very necessary, however they should have been paid for by tax increases and reduced spending. Instead we have had tax cuts and increased consumer and government spending. It doesn't take a degree in rocket science to figure out that there is a serious imbalance taking place.

Of course the government debt just adds fuel to the fire. Even though government debt does not have a maximum ceiling, it is still contributing to the economic downturn. The Chinese, the Japanese, and the Europeans are primary lenders to the United States. As the value of the dollar continues to drop against their currencies, they are losing money on their investments. Now they are insisting on raising the interest rates on those loans to make their money back. The result of these interest rate hikes will cause everyone in America to have higher loan payments. This is simply because as interest rates increase, interest payments increase. As the debt burden is increased on consumers it will force them to reduce spending. Then the government has only two options: borrow more money or raise taxes. At this point if the government tries to reduce spending by reducing the number of people that are employed by the government, it will further the economic downturn because more people will be unemployed.

One of the major issues with correcting our current problems is the fact that manufacturing and innovation have seen large declines over the past twenty years. Most companies have been tweaking their bottom lines instead of investing for future business. This will make it harder for American companies to compete with the world in new technologies. In fact I don't see any new innovative technologies in the making ready to be launched out to rescue us from our despair. In the past century we have seen some world-changing inventions come on the scene that had a major impact on consumers and industry. Some of these include telephones, radios, automobiles, airplanes, televisions, microchips, computers, and the Internet. Now it seems like the focus has been on making things faster. While this is good it is highly unlikely to result in a huge advantage for consumers and businesses in the long run. Of course just because we haven't seen any major breakthrough technologies emerge in recent years doesn't mean that there won't be any. However for this to take place there must be a change in the priority of industry. The overwhelming priority in recent years has been to make profits look superficially good.

Every time there is a slowdown in the economy companies respond with sudden layoffs to offset their expenses. Next they will raise prices for their goods or services to maintain profits. The solution to their dilemmas, which would be to expand and go after new business, will not be done. After all even in good economic times it is safer and easier to make a demand on current people and businesses. Then they will use more creative accounting to make bottom lines look good.

I strongly believe that debt will be the trigger to cause the next crash. The information I am sharing with you is not new; it is just that now it is more pertinent and real than ever before. This is because of the extreme decline in the savings rate and the consumer debt nearing maximum capacity. Then like a thief in the night the excess we have been living in for the past 20 years will begin to consume us. It is not the government's fault or the terrorists' fault, although many people would like to put the blame on them. As a matter of fact few people are exempt from responsibility, and even fewer will be exempt from the coming economic hurt.

Of course as in all times of hardship there will be several glimmers of hope given to the economy. The stock analysts will continue to assure people that the stock market has hit the bottom and that it can only go up. People will buy into it, especially those that maintain the buy and hold philosophy. They will say it will come back, only to be disappointed when it doesn't.

A depression is just what it sounds like. Depressions always seem to sink further and further down almost in a self-inflicting way. As unemployment goes up, companies get weaker and are forced to cut more jobs, which just adds to the unemployment. Due to the high unemployment rate consumer spending will come to a halt, which will cause company profits to decrease. Slowly people will lose faith in the markets and sell stock, which will cause the market to decline even further.

The housing market is another problem area in a coming depression. In recent years many people took out adjustable rate mortgages and bought houses with either no collateral or very little collateral. As unemployment soars and the cost of living increases people will be forced to default on these mortgage loans. This will force banks to foreclose on the houses and sell them, causing a surge of homes on the market, which will lead to a deflation of home values. In this scenario the banks stand to be the ones most affected. As home values decline consumers who can't make their payments will willingly give back their homes to the banks. Without the help of the federal government in this situation banks will fold. The reason for this is that banks got overconfident and didn't counterbalance the risk they were taking with marginal mortgage loans.

The auto market will also see its fair share of hardship during the next Great Depression. Over the past seven years automakers have been ramping up on the production of new SUVs, also known as gas-guzzlers. However in a depression people want to reduce their cost of living any way they can. This means they will opt for more gas-conservative automobiles. Detroit isn't ready for this move because of the major emphasis on these SUVs. This will create major layoffs in the automobile industry. On top of the layoffs the under funded pension funds will be gone. Instead of Detroit getting all of the business, the Japanese, with their high mileage cars, will be the ones to capitalize.

The war in Iraq isn't helping much with our economic status as a whole. In fact I don't think that it is a war that can be won by military force. It has turned more into a civil war with religion being the focal point than anything else. The American soldiers are right in the middle of it and it will only get worse. The violence between the Shiites, Sunnis, and Kurds will continue to escalate, which will lead to higher death tolls than ever. Costs to be involved in this conflict are going to skyrocket. It will become much like the Vietnam War era with anti-war marches and protests taking place across the States. I believe that Congress is getting fed up and will soon refuse to continue to fund the war. The White House will be forced to pull out and bring the soldiers home. This will most likely be met with a takeover of Iraq by the Anti-American Iranian government. Even though the economic problems we are currently facing started during the Clinton era, Bush will undoubtedly catch the brunt of the blame. The tax cuts and the wars on terror and in Iraq have only fueled the problems.

Continuing on the path of no return the United States Government will fall into some serious trouble. Unfortunately at this point, anything the United States Government tries to do to remedy the problem will be met with heavy resistance because we'll be into the depression with so much debt. Even if the United States raises interest rates on treasury bonds considerably we will still be faced with trouble because of the large debts we have incurred. Of course the only other alternative will be to print more money. The Fed has already stated publicly that they will do this before they will ever allow deflation. Of course this will only translate into worldwide turmoil in the financial markets.

This next election period will be a key election in the destiny of our nation. If the Democrats win it will be a different Democratic party than we've seen. This will be due to reduced tax income, and Democrats will be forced to reduce spending across the board, including social programs. At this point the government will have to downsize which will lead to massive job layoffs. Foreign countries will force us to write a balanced budget plan before they loan us any more money. Just as we have treated nations with out-of-control economies in the past, so will we be treated.

Social Security will be another dilemma during this time. The only logical solution will be to immediately change the retirement age to 70, since this will reduce Social Security retirement costs starting the following year. The birth rate will go to nearly zero and abortions will increase at a rapid rate.

Eventually the debt problem will begin to diminish because with inflated dollars, both the consumer debt and the government debt will seem smaller, and they will be paid back with a dollar worth far less than it is now. Of course every country that has loaned money to the U.S. or every individual who bought inflation adjusted bonds or saved money in a bank will all be on the losing side of this scenario.

The United States will turn from a very complex society into a more simple society. Instead of our lives being driven with the ambition to have more we will find ourselves enjoying the more simple things of life. I can go on and on explaining things that could happen in this depression. However that is not the true purpose of this book. I just want you to have an idea that things can get bad. That is why right now as an individual you should be reflecting on your habits of spending and saving like never before. You can make adjustments right now that can help you if in fact a depression does occur in the near future. Later on in the book I will go into some specific things that you can do to prepare for this type of environment.

CHAPTER 6

More Causes for Depression

Everything about our global economy is changing, and that includes the U.S. dollar. If we look back in history we can see that past events have affected everything. The Black Death for instance created a devastating labor shortage that rocked Europe for decades. Christopher Columbus' voyage turned trade upside down for centuries. And of course in more recent years the industrial revolution moved economic powers in ways that continue to affect the economy to this day. Now we're facing another great shift away from the U.S. dollar dominance of world markets, making way for new leaders like China and India.

We are in a place right now where one simple trigger can send our economy into another economic depression. I have already identified what I believe to be the main culprit, which is debt. However there are other factors that if triggered could just as easily send us into another economic depression. I honestly do not think that we will see the full effects of these problems come to an apex until the year 2010 or 2011. Just know that it is on the horizon.

An Unstoppable Force

What about the so-called "Boomer Bomb?" In case you don't know what that is let me explain it. In 2008 the leading-edge boomers, born in 1946, turn 62. In case you were wondering how old you have to be to start collecting social security the current answer is 62.

So the "Boomer Bomb" is when 77 million ex- hippie, disco-dancing Americans start moving into retirement. This is a serious dilemma because they will move into retirement expecting to be completely taken care of and find that they are instead completely unfunded and unprepared.

But what will happen will not only effect the Boomer generation but anyone else who is in the middle class society as well. Just imagine how much havoc this could actually wreak. Imagine policy changes that:

1. Immediately and permanently double your federal income taxes.
2. Immediately and permanently hike your state taxes by at least 15%.
3. Immediately and permanently slash your Social Security benefits by half.
4. Immediately and permanently eliminate half of your annual Medicare benefits.
5. Immediately and permanently wipe out half of every military pension check.

What I am describing to you is not an alternative. Peter Peterson, former White House economic adviser says, "Absent a colliding comet or an alien invasion, this will surely happen." Simply put there is no way for American investors to avoid such a collapse.

With 77 million babies born between 1946 and 1964 the baby boomers have long been the force behind the economic trends of our nation in recent history. At times this has been great for the American economy and at other times it has forced us into a deadly trap that has caused millions of Americans to go broke. I believe right now is one of those "go broke" times for many Americans.

Take a look at the following chart. It shows that we are living longer.

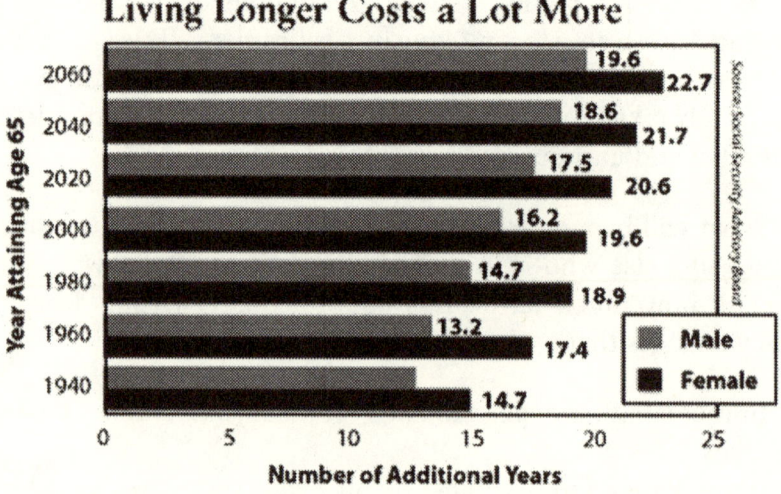

Living Longer Costs a Lot More

Source: Social Security Advisory Board

Of course living longer sounds like great news to many people, but it can have some very negative effects on our economy. In fact people have always been in search of ways to live longer. But we already have 10 times more people over the age of 65 than we did at the turn of the last century. In fact the fastest growing age group in America are those over 85 years of age. So all of this equates to there being more than a 300% gain in people over 85 than we have right now.

The bottom line reality on all of this information is that the longer you live the more money you need. To obtain more money you need a stronger stock portfolio, better and less expensive health insurance and access to a trust fund that is much larger than the one currently set up by Washington.

From now until 2040 the Census Bureau estimates almost double the number of people ages 65-74 and more than triple the number of people over age 85. We'll even have 13 times as many people living past 100.

By 2030 costs for nursing homes alone will exceed what we now spend on Social Security. Total Medicare payments will have to soar 6 times as high and Social Security payments will need to double to sustain this type of growth.

You say but won't the next generation be able to take care of this just as the baby boomers have taken care of their elderly parents? The answer is a definite no. The reason is quite simple. Take a look at the next chart and I believe you will see why.

More Grandmas Than Grandchildren

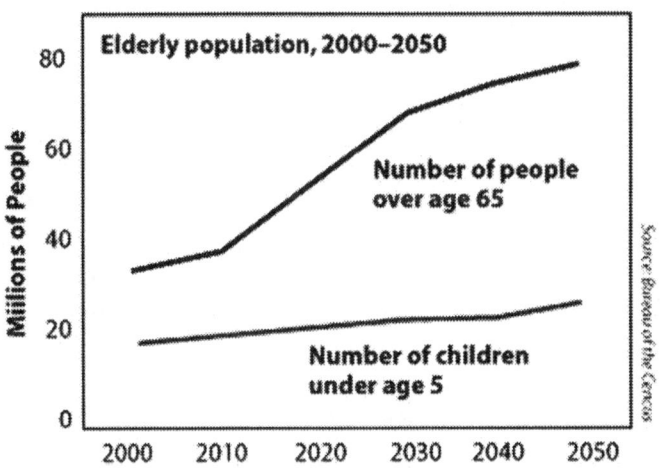

Suddenly the birth rate in America has decreased and we are now left with a baby shortage to take care of the rising elderly population. So what is the culprit? Better use of birth control is the main one, along with women who have pursued careers instead of raising children. The statistics are astounding. In 1980 nearly 10% of American women ended their childbearing years without giving birth. Today it has almost doubled to more than 19%. Most women who will have children will on average have two. This is the figure given by the Census Bureau to keep a population from shrinking.

So by 2030 the numbers of over 65 Americans (Retirees) will more than double while the number of younger Americans (Workers) will stay pretty flat. This is a rising trend that is not just a scenario that may happen, it absolutely is happening. For example, fifty years ago the public cost for supporting each retiree was divided among 16.5 workers. Today that number has fallen to a staggering 3.4 workers.

This leads us to a grim outlook for the younger generation as well. The problem with the baby boomer generation is that most of them are middle class. Even worse they are often called the "sandwich generation," forced between paying for their kids' rising college tuitions and footing the bill for their elderly parents. Few have enough money left over to create any real retirement savings. All of this combined with our credit-crazy culture spells disaster.

But it is not just the baby boomers that will suffer financially. Remember how we established that the baby boomers have set many trends in our economy since the '60s? Well they're about to establish another one that will affect everyone else who is dependent on the boomer trends. This includes investors, homebuilders, domestic companies, and the average American citizen.

The major dilemma the boomers face is their looming retirement dates. When they retire they will need enough financial stability to continue their lifestyle. They won't be able to get this done just on Social Security.

First of all they will need a lot more savings than what they currently have. This is something that we have already talked about to some degree but it is crucial to their retirement. Houses could count as savings, however in this last housing boom created by extremely low interest rates many baby boomers took out the max mortgage they could. This is a serious problem especially as house prices begin to deflate from their current levels. They will actually be upside down and in serious debt.

So what are the exact figures of the deteriorating savings rate? Well let me tell you what some of our neighbors are saving. The average Japanese citizen saves about 15% of annual income. In Europe the figure is around 10%. We have already mentioned China has a savings rate of 25%. In direct contrast the Average American has a savings rate of less than 1% and as if it could get any worse it is declining even more. Some analysts estimate that it will be in the negative by the beginning of 2007!

Of course adding to the falling savings rate is the decline of many boomers' portfolios. Some have dropped as much as 40% in recent years. Add to this the fact that many of them have had near stagnant wages for most of their working lives and you have a mixture that creates intense poverty for many people.

So some of the Boomers have taken some hits in the financial market, but what about the one third that have absolutely zero savings, zero investments and zero pensions? Those percentages total about 25 million U.S. households with average net assets of less than $1,000.

To add to the lack of savings of most boomers is the cost of living. In the past two decades most things have doubled and tripled in cost while wages have not grown proportionately. When you add inflation into the mix, since 1975 real wages have only increased by 1.2%.

Again some people will argue the fact that their house has doubled or tripled in value in the past 5 years. The bleak reality is that they will not stay there forever and in fact the bust is coming sooner than most people think.

House prices have inflated considerably in recent years but the main problem with that is that most of the people who own them have taken out second mortgages and now owe 100% of the value. In 2005 alone mortgage debt rose by $885 billion.

The average house price has increased by 50% in the last 5 years on a national level. However, wages have stagnated leaving more and more people unable to afford houses at new inflated prices. This is where the deception lies in what may become the greatest housing crash of our history.

Soaring house prices are not a sign of soaring riches. This is because housing prices did not increase proportionate to income. In other words, housing prices are not a reflection of a great financial increase. Rather they are increasing because of lower rates making it more affordable for people to buy, but also making it easier for less credit-worthy borrowers to obtain high-risk financing. Cap it off with the increased amount of adjustable rate mortgages and interest only loans and you have a bust waiting to happen.

Interest-only loans are loans in which you only are required to pay the interest payment for a given number of years, usually ten. Up front these mortgages seem great because they increase your cash flow and allow you to qualify for a home that you would otherwise not be able to afford. The kicker is when you have to begin to pay the principal payments and you haven't paid down your balance. Most people's philosophy is that they will move in 10 years. What if you can't sell your house because it is worth less than what you owe? This is exactly what is going to happen to many Americans in the near future.

Living on Borrowed Time?

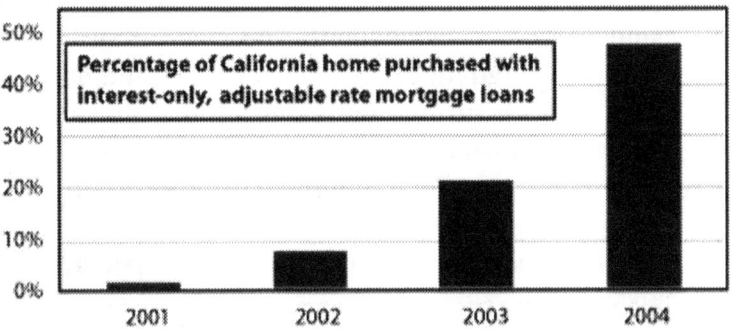

On top of the mortgage debt the average American household has over $8,000 in credit card debt at 19% interest. When interest rates rise and these credit card companies require payment where will the money come from? People will default on their obligations, which will not only cause house prices to plummet, but it will also become so hard to obtain credit due to high interest rates it will be ridiculous. These defaults will effect everyone including businesses that need credit to expand or to maintain until they can expand. The only two solutions to this problem will be for people to default or for the wages to soar to cover the difference in payments. The latter solution is highly unlikely.

Federal Reserve Chairman Ben Bernanke recently said that, "unless the current generation is willing to sacrifice, by cutting consumption or increasing savings, future generations could face a heavier reduction in living standards."

So as we can see the future savings prospect for boomer retirees looks pretty grim. No savings, no wage hikes, and no clear future for real estate. So this brings about another problem: How is this cash-strapped boomer going pay for an unexpected expense like a medical emergency? Unfortunately for the boomer, private insurance is covering less and less. Who will be forced to pay for the huge hospital bill of the baby boomers? The only likely source will be America's younger taxpayers.

Fed Chairman Bernanke also stated recently that Congress could not avoid hard choices to reform what he called "unsustainable" Medicare and Social Security benefits. If Congress shores up the programs solely through higher revenue, taxes would have to rise by 25% by 2030, with further increases needed down the line. Funding the programs solely by cutting other federal spending would require about $700 billion in reductions by 2030.

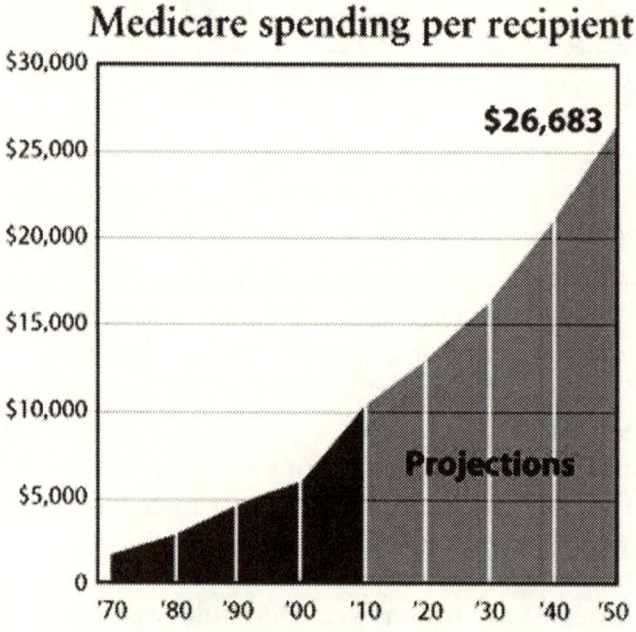

Medicare spending per recipient

One of the reasons medical expenses are soaring is because we have the best medical care in the world. The only way for us to have it is to spend money. For instance, drug companies currently spend as much as the Pentagon on research. But the rest of the medical industry spends even more. There are the MRIs, the CAT scans, biomedicine and implants.

That leaves us to reason that the older Americans will want the most advanced healthcare. Why? Well we have already said that people since the beginning of time have been trying to learn how to live longer. And no one wants to be sick.

The problem with that is that the most advanced medical care is very expensive. Right now at present-day rates it costs four times more to take care of an individual over 65 as it does to cover medical expenses for a younger adult.

But then again who really cares when you are sick? Medicare and Medicaid can always pick up the expenses, right? Well the costs for Medicaid and Medicare are growing faster than that of even Social Security. About eight times faster, depending upon whose figures you look at.

Healthcare costs are soaring faster than the costs of just about everything except oil. To add to all of these expenses, parents from the previous generation are growing older and either moving into nursing homes or are moving in with their boomer children. In many cases this forces the boomers to spend their savings on nursing homes or care for their elderly parents.

Whatever costs come out of the boomers' pockets they take out of their own retirement plans. Gaps in coverage and healthcare affordability are wide open and growing even wider.

Unfortunately many boomers will not have savings enough to cover those gaps. As a result many companies will not be able to provide adequate healthcare to their employees and many individuals will not be able to afford healthcare. Already the middle class citizen is often the one stuck without healthcare.

Terrorists

This seems to be one of the most likely factors that could trigger an economic depression. The problem with the terrorist attacks is that they are a great unknown. They can literally strike at any time unawares. This leaves us with a huge time gap in this theory because we don't know if and when it will ever happen. The U.S. Government and Homeland Security said it is more of a when than if. In other words they agree that another terrorist attack is inevitable. They just don't know where or when. The scary thing about the terrorists is that they are very patient. They are willing to wait as long as it takes to carry out their plans.

Some speculation as to what the terrorists would most likely attack has been in play for some time now. As seen in the 2001 World Trade Center attack they wanted to go for the backbone of our financial strength. This will probably be what they try to attack again. One industry that we know is vulnerable is our oil refineries. A brief interruption in our oil supply could have serious effects on our economy and a more long-term interruption would be devastating.

Oil Supply & Energy Prices

The price of standard crude oil on NYMEX was under $25/barrel in September 2003. By August 11, 2005, the price had been above $60/barrel for over a week and a half. A record price of $78.40 per barrel was reached on July 13, 2006, due in part to North Korea's missile launches, the Middle East Crisis, Iranian nuclear brinkmanship and reports from the U.S Department of Energy showing a decline in petroleum reserves. While oil prices are considerably higher than a year ago, they are still roughly $14 from exceeding the inflation-adjusted peak of the 1980 shock, when prices were over $90 a barrel in today's prices.

In the United States gasoline prices reached an all-time high during the first week of September 2005 in the aftermath of Hurricane Katrina. The average retail price was nearly $3.04 per gallon. The previous high was $2.38 per gallon in March 1981, which would be $3.20 per gallon after adjustment for inflation.

There are a number of reasons why oil traders feel that oil supplies might be reduced. One of the most important is growing turbulence in the Middle East, the world's largest oil-producing region. The war in Iraq, Iran's nuclear program, and internal instability in Saudi Arabia could all lead to a dramatic fall in the supply of oil. Outside the Middle East other oil producers with their own issues have caused worry for investors, such as the strikes and political problems in Venezuela and potential instability in West Africa.

In late August 2005, Hurricane Katrina crippled the supply-flow from offshore rigs in the Gulf Coast, the largest source of oil for the domestic U.S. market. Short-term shutdowns because of power outages knocked out two major on-shore pipelines, and at least 10% of the nation's refining capacity was not operating in the wake of the storm. Gas prices in the region, normally 70 cents below the national average, were at $3.12 on August 30.

World supply came in at 83 million barrels a day during 2004 in Department of Energy EIA calculations. This rate of increase is faster than that of any other date in the past. Despite this increase in supply, prices have continued to rise, leading to increasing discussion of peak oil and the possibility that the future may see a reduced supply of oil.

Even if oil supplies themselves are not reduced, some experts feel the easily accessible sources of light sweet crude are almost exhausted and in the future the world will depend on more expensive sources of heavy oil and alternatives.

The short-term price of oil is partially controlled by the OPEC cartel and the oligopoly of major oil companies. One other important cause is the United States dollar's slump against the euro. Since oil is traded in dollars, the price must increase for OPEC to maintain purchasing power in Europe.

As the dollar's rate of exchange continues to fall against the world's major currencies, there has been much speculation about the likely knock-on effect. One area receiving a lot of attention is crude oil in general, and OPEC in particular.

It has been suggested that OPEC may begin pricing crude oil in terms of the euro, and further, that OPEC may actually begin invoicing its crude oil exports in terms of euros. This latter step would require shifting out of dollars, with OPEC receiving euros in payment. If this happened in the major oil exporting nations we could see severe consequences for the dollar.

Over the past 30 years the United States has been losing control of its energy supply. This has had a negative effect on our economy by making it vulnerable to external political and economic factors. Before 1973, when the United States produced most of the oil it consumed, the relationship between economic growth and inflation followed a clear pattern. If the economy grew substantially inflation would grow also. The government would keep it in check by raising the interest rates and tightening the money supply, which would in turn slow down the economy. Then when the economy cooled off enough they would lower the rates again to stimulate economic growth. But then in the 1970s we saw a strange thing happen which caused the pattern of economics in our nation to change. It would become known as Hubbert's Law.

During the 1950s there was a geophysicist by the name of M. King Hubbert who observed that once you extract half the oil from a given field, production begins to decline. In regards to the United States, Hubbert concluded that America's oil production would peak in the early 1970s.

If we look back at the 1970s we can clearly see that Hubbert's prediction came true. In 1970 U.S. oil production reached its all time maximum production capacity of 9 million barrels per day. Since then we have seen a slow decline in this production capacity. Today, the nation only produces about 5 million barrels per day. In addition to the slowed production the 1970s also marked the first time the United States began consuming more imported oil than domestically produced oil. Foreign oil use has been on the rise ever since.

In 1973, America showed forth its new weakness when the OPEC nations imposed restrictions on oil exports, causing a 70% increase in global oil prices. Then OPEC forced oil prices even higher by imposing a total embargo on oil exports. Because of the spike in oil prices the American economy fell under serious pressure, resulting in a new type of problem known as stagflation.

In stagflation growth stagnated and inflation rose at the same time. This created an issue for the government. They couldn't figure out what to do to cure the problem. Should it raise interest rates to fight inflation, or lower rates to restore growth? It could not do both, which was a dilemma that created the worst economic time our nation has seen since the 1930s.

Of course we know the rest of the story. Things cooled off in the Middle East and oil prices fell. This was not only made possible by the OPEC nations though. Non-OPEC nations such as the United Kingdom and Europe helped level things out by increasing oil production. However in 1999 we saw a new change come about that may be even more serious than the decreased domestic production of oil. Oil production from non-OPEC nations appeared to reach its maximum level and may have even declined.

This creates a serious problem for the United States because in order to experience continued economic growth and status we will require more amounts of energy than ever before. Right now oil is the source for that energy and will most likely continue to be the source well into the near future. More oil coming from the allies that helped us out previously is also a very limited chance. So whom must we depend on? The only ones I see will be our Middle Eastern neighbors.

Saudi Arabia seems the most likely source for this increased oil production. After all they are our staunchest Middle Eastern ally. But who is to say that Saudi Arabia can or even will provide us with the oil that we need to continue to run things at full peak? After all no one knows for sure how much oil Saudi Arabia actually has.

But even graver than this situation is the political situation that we are facing in the Middle East. Although Saudi Arabia is our strongest ally they still have to be very careful what business they conduct. The powerful religious establishment in Saudi Arabia, which practices the Wahhabi form of Sunni Islam, is very anti-American.

So it seems that the only ones who can support America with more oil are the ones whose populations exhibit the strongest anti-American sentiment in the world. Even nations like Venezuela, Nigeria, and the former Soviet Union would be opposed to helping us. We don't exactly have the best foreign relations with any of these nations either.

On the other hand Great Britain and Europe, who have come to our aid in the past, may not be able to step up production if things get tough. And even though Britain is our ally in the war on terror and the wars in Iraq and Afghanistan, the majority of the population is largely opposed to the campaign.

So why aren't we vigorously pursuing alternative energy? After all this could be one of the next major breakthroughs that could positively impact our economy for years to come. It almost seems as if we have put all of our eggs in one basket and refuse to go look for any more. Alternative energy should be our top priority, but our society and our leaders have failed to realize two very important things. One is that just because oil has always been plentiful it will not always be plentiful. Most civilizations throughout history have actually collapsed due to the limited production of a crucial resource. This is the risk we take when our dependence for energy lies in oil alone.

They have also assumed that there is no alternative to oil that is worth pursuing. That is simply not true.

Much of our society is unwilling to face the reality that gas stations may not always offer gas at the pumps 24/7. They are blinded to the fact that oil production will eventually decrease and we will eventually exhaust our supply. This will of course have a significant effect on society as we know it today.

Even more serious than what we have already previously pointed out is the fact that the world's demand for oil is growing faster than oil production can increase. Some petroleum geologists believe that oil production worldwide is at its permanent long-term peak and may be close to starting a permanent decline. At the same time demand for oil is increasing, especially from large developing nations like China and India. I believe that this trend of oil supply and demand will continue which will inevitably send oil prices sky high.

This will have a severe impact on our economy. In Europe people have been paying $6 per gallon for several years. But America has never seen gas prices of much more than $3 per gallon. What would $10 a gallon gas do to the majority of our society? People wouldn't be able to afford to drive to work. Gas shortages would become regular occurrences. Energy prices would soar and people would not be able to afford to keep the lights on. These are all real situations that could happen in the near future.

Inflation

In mainstream economics, inflation is a rise in the general level of prices, as measured against some baseline of purchasing power. The prevailing view in mainstream economics is that inflation is caused by the interaction of the supply of money with output and interest rates.

Inflation is the bull chasing the man with the red cape on. Unfortunately America is that man. This bull will probably demonstrate his terror by driving the debt bubble into unmanageable levels. The Fed is already raising short-term interest rates, which are having an effect on credit cards and home equity loans. Also the CMT (Constant Maturity Treasury) rate is increasing which will have a negative impact on adjustable rate mortgages. Add this to the declining value of the dollar against other world currencies, which will make imports more expensive, and you have a very ripe environment for inflation.

Everything is pointing towards inflation. In the 1970s the inflation rate was well over 10% for many years, which had a major impact on people on fixed incomes. As a result many investments suffered considerably.

The other argument for the coming depression is that we will experience a deflation. However, I do not believe that we will experience this type of economic environment in the coming depression. The first reason why I will make this argument is based upon what we know the Federal Reserve has already expressed. In 2002, the Fed's then governor Benjamin Bernanke, who just happens to be the chairman now, announced that they would print more money before allowing deflation to happen. What's worse is that The Fed no longer tells the public how much money they are printing. You can be sure of this though: they are printing huge amounts. How do I know? For one thing we have been managing to send hundreds of billions of dollars overseas to Europe and Asia for years now. Where are all of these hundreds of billions of dollars coming from? Straight from the printing presses.

This can have some very negative side effects. First of all currency maintains its value only by its relative scarcity. This is even truer for currencies that are not backed by gold, which has been the case with the U.S. dollar since 1968, when Nixon pulled the final plug on the gold standard. The bottom line without getting too complicated is this: the more currency that is in the market, the more its value goes down, which leads to inflation.

The second most probable reason for inflation rather than deflation is the fact that unlike the 1929 depression, industry has not increased capacity for many years. The government has not been able to convince industry that the economy is turning around and will soon begin to grow. As a result, even if they have seen an increase in demand, they have not added more employees, but rather have opted to work their current employees harder or outsource to other countries.

Of course, as we have already discussed in greater depth in the previous chapter, real estate will be the exception to inflation. The reason for that is that housing prices in many areas are already severely inflated. We are in a housing bubble that is about to pop. I believe this will be quite dramatic in many markets. The good news is that it will probably only take a short time for this deflation to correct itself. A few years are what I mean by a short time. Why is this good news? Well its not good news for everyone, but those who have been diligent savers and who are going to invest in the right things over the next 3-5 years will have a great opportunity to tap into in the real estate market.

Inflation may not be the single most important key to trigger another depression but it definitely is a player.

What about China?

The recent buzz from the Fed and the U.S. manufacturing industry has been pinning the blame for the U.S. trade deficit on China's undervalued currency, accusing them of stealing jobs and dumping goods. Although some of the claims are true to a certain extent, a yuan revaluation would certainly not be the rescue package that saves the dollar from its recent troubles. Unfortunately for the dollar a revaluation of the yuan will be a depreciation of the dollar against the yuan along with other world currencies whose central banks will dump their reserves of U.S. dollars. That brings us to the economic effects that this nominal exchange rate change implies. The dollar's recent stumble is largely due to its record-breaking current account deficit. Although in the short run, a yuan revaluation might cause an improvement of the trade situation with China, it's not likely that this will last. Because of sticky wages and prices, Chinese consumers will buy more American products after a revaluation because their income will be worth more in terms of the dollars that they pay. This will cause a small and temporary decline in the U.S. trade deficit, which will mean good news for dollar bulls. However as prices, and consequently foreign demand, adjust in the medium term, the negative effects on China's export industry will be felt in the economy as a whole. Chinese wages should decline and consumption of both foreign and domestic goods will slow during a period of adjustment causing a downward deviation from the current inflationary trend.

Lower prices combined with an elevated currency value means that, in real exchange rate terms, China's price competitiveness would move towards pre-revaluation levels again. This being said, keep in mind that, as shown in U.S. trade data for the first half of 2004, China is the destination for only a little over 4% of U.S. exports and it's the origin of slightly under 13% of U.S. imports. All in all, the short term price effect of the revaluation will be muted by the income effect in the longer run, which leaves the dollar worse off and facing the same depreciation pressures as before.

CHAPTER 7

Wealth or Poverty?
It's Your Choice

By now if you are not where you think you should be in regards to your wealth building system, then what I have been sharing with you has probably been striking fear deep into your heart. I don't like the emotions that come with fear so understand that it is not my intention to make you afraid. But fear, if used correctly, can motivate you to change.

My own analysis of fear is that it will cause you to do one of two things. Fear of loss is either the force that paralyzes you or it is the force that becomes your greatest motivator for gain. Those are the two options that you have at this point. You can feel hopeless like there is nothing that you can do about what is coming or you can overcome that and begin to take the necessary steps to accomplish your financial goals.

I will tell you this, now is not the time to squander everything you have on self-gratifying pleasures that feed your "now" hunger. It is a time to pay off your debt and begin to save like never before.

Of course there will be those of you that do not believe what I have said and that is fine. But let me ask you this: what do you have to lose by taking my advice? Absolutely nothing. On the contrary if you don't take my advice you could lose everything.

Relying on bureaucrats to save Social Security and Medicare or the mutual fund manager to redirect your investments is just too dangerous. The global forces shaping these events are too large for them to manage. And their incentive to fix the problems are just not in line with your own needs as an investor.

That really only leaves you with one option. You must aggressively save and build your own system of financial security and savvy investing for the rocky times ahead. That is exactly what the remainder of this book is going to show you how to do.

You have probably heard a financial advisor or seen a TV show or read a book that teaches you how to budget your money. That is not what these last pages are about. Although I will say this: you need to aggressively cut your spending, cut down as much debt as you possibly can, and save the rest. Unless you are raking in more money than you could possibly spend, I would take this advice very seriously.

So if you do take my advice and save that is great. But let me ask you where are you going to put the money you save and what are you going to do with your current investments, if you have any? Are you going to bury your spare cash in your back yard or put it under your mattress? That's probably not the smartest thing to do, so you need to know where to invest your savings.

Of course you always want to have cash savings. I am not just talking about a bank savings account either. I am talking about cold hard cash that you keep in a safe in your house. Why? Because cash is king. For instance you all remember the Hurricane Katrina disaster that struck our nation in late 2005. Did you know that people who lived in the areas that got hit could not access money in their bank accounts for up to two weeks? If you don't have any cash in that kind of situation it could become very troublesome.

What if there were a nuclear terrorist attack around the area where you live? Chances are unless you are in the direct blast path (25 mile radius) you will live and you will probably be able to get to safety. But more than likely the banking system in your area would get hit very hard and it might not be possible for you to get cash out of your account or to even use your credit cards. That is why cash is important.

The main reason why cash is not a good place to keep a majority of your money is very simple. It is not a sound investment. By that I simply mean that it will more than likely not gain in value over time. Especially in an inflationary environment. I believe, as we talked about in the previous chapter, inflation will be impossible to avoid in the coming economic depression.

Now by cash investment most people understand that we are talking about savings accounts, CDs, T-bills, and other short-term deposits. Usually the way these safe investments work is to make up losses by paying low levels of interest that balance out losses due to inflation. However in the inflationary period of the 1970s interest rates paid on cash were less than the inflation rate. So even though you would have added more dollars to your savings account through the interest collected, it would have been worth less. 10.5% less to be exact.

Currently, the yield on three month T-bills is 5.04 percent and the inflation rate is estimate at 4.5 percent. So let me ask you. Would you like to earn .54 percent on your money? Or better yet would .54 percent on your money help you when it comes to your retirement? Probably not.

If you are looking to secure your financial future cash is not the way to go.

Table 1* How Cash Holdings Performed in the 1970s

	Average annual nominal returns	Average annual real returns	Total real returns	Change in real $10,000
Cash	5.5%	-1.9%	-17.5%	$8,250

This leads us to the next investment that you should steer clear of at this point: bonds. Bonds are a very popular and traditional investment among retirees and those seeking income. A bond is a loan to a government or a corporation that must be paid back when it matures. Bonds are a better investment than cash, and they are usually more stable than stocks. However, they do not do well in inflationary periods in the economy. That is why I do not recommend these investments today.

Bonds work in the following way. When an investor lends money, they require that the income they get from the loan equals the inflation rate plus a reasonable amount of interest. So naturally, the higher the inflation rate, the higher the yield on bonds.

The negative to this is that price and yield on bonds move in the opposite direction. As the yield on bonds goes up the price goes down and vice versa. During inflation yields normally go up in order to cool down the economy. So generally the higher the inflation rate, the higher the yield on bonds.

For example, say that you own a bond that pays you 5.04 percent annual interest. With inflation at 4.5 percent, your bond only pays you .54 percent in real terms. Now let's say that inflation rises to 8.2 percent in the next 2 years. What happened? The yield on the bond became inverted to the inflation rate and now you are losing value. So naturally, if you try and sell your bond the purchaser will want compensation for the increase in inflation. Of course the new purchaser is going to want the yield from the bond to be about 3.7 percent higher. Guess who loses in this situation? You. Why? Because the only way for the new purchaser to get the higher yield is for him to pay you a lower price for the bond.

During the 1970s when inflation reached well over 10 percent, bond prices fell on average by 1.9% a year. I believe that during the period of inflation we are moving into bonds will mirror the 1970s but probably much worse.

Table 2* Performance of Bonds in the 1970s

	Average annual nominal return	Average annual real return	Total real returns	Change in real $10,000
Bonds	5.5%	-1.9%	-17.5%	$8,250

Now, let's talk serious business. Everyone always wants to know about the stock market. The biggest reason for that is because of the very large gains the stock market saw for the better part of the 90s. Most investors see the stock market as the best, or sometimes the only investment vehicle. Financial advisors shout diversification, but let me ask you what exactly are they diversifying into? More mutual funds? Stocks? Large-cap, small-cap? These are all investments that the so-called experts tell you are your best bet. Why? Well, they say it is because the stock market always rebounds.

But how do stocks perform during inflation? Let's take a look. During the '70s when inflation was high only certain stocks fared well. But overall the market will perform poorly and some segments will suffer serious losses.

The S&P grew by only 5.9% a year during the '70s period of inflation. But inflation grew by over 7% per year, so the real return loss for the decade was 14 percent. The stock market of the 1930s, the era of the Great Depression, did not even see this. Stocks during this period still gained 20 percent in real terms during this time.

So I am recommending that you stay out of the index investments. Stay away from the funds that diversify into indexes, large-cap stocks, and all other broad market diversification. This will only damage your portfolio.

Table 3* How Large-Cap Stocks Performed in 1970s

	Average annual nominal return	Average annual real returns	Total real returns	Change in real $10,000
S&P 500	5.9%	-1.5%	-14.0%	$8,600

One effect of inflation is that it causes price/earnings ratios to fall clear across the board. The primary reason for this is due in large part to the uncertainty that comes during periods of high inflation. Businesses are not confident enough to grow during periods of high inflation. They are not as optimistic about the future during these times. Investors feel the same way. The uncertainty makes investors leery of paying higher prices for shares in companies because no one knows how high future prices will be. Thus the P/E ratios fall.

The other reason why P/E ratios fall is two-fold. It deals with earnings growth, which comes from expansion, and inflationary growth, which comes from having to charge higher prices to cover higher costs. Most investors do not put a high value on inflationary growth, because it applies equally to all companies. The value that investors put on real growth is extremely high, because it comes from proper management.

Earnings growth that expressly comes from inflationary growth will cause P/E ratios to fall because investors will not want to pay as much for that type of growth.

This is why the stock investments typically viewed as safe haven stocks, which obtain their profits whether in good time or bad, will perform poorly. These include products such as food, household goods, and personal care items. Demand for these products stays fairly consistent whether in good times or bad, which causes them to usually have high P/E ratios.

This will be damaging to these particular types of stocks in the coming years because periods of high inflation cause price/earnings ratios to decline dramatically. In the 1970s when P/E ratios declined from 16 to 8 in the S&P 500, retail stores, food stocks, and cosmetics all underperformed. Cosmetic stocks are the ones that got hit the hardest in this group with a loss of 45.6%.

Still, the hardest to be hit will be companies whose profits are inversely related to energy prices. The airlines, automakers, and chemical manufacturers will be the ones to suffer the most. These groups suffered huge losses during the 1970s and I suspect it will be even graver this time around. The table below shows you how companies in these sectors performed during the '70s.

Stocks Whose Profits are Inversely Related to Energy
1970 High to 1979 low

Sectors	Nominal Changes
Airlines	-37.0%
Autos	-55.0%
Chemicals	-47.3%

Small-Cap Stocks
Table 4* How Small-Cap Stocks Performed 1970s

	Average annual nominal returns	Average annual real returns	Total real returns	Change in real $10,000
Small-cap stocks	11.6%	4.2%	50.9%	$15,090

As seen by the table above small-caps performed pretty well during the 1970s when inflation was high. Long-term studies have actually proven that they tend to do better than large-cap stocks overall.

Small-caps have a large advantage over large-cap stocks that helps them to outperform. Generally speaking they can usually grow their earnings at a faster rate. This is because it only takes a small amount of revenues for a small-cap company to achieve serious growth, whereas a company with $100 million in revenues must come up with ways to significantly increase their revenues to see only a small amount of growth. This is why even in the inflation of the 1970s small-cap companies were able to counter lower P/E ratios, which resulted in better earnings.

This time around it will not be so easy. The main reason is because smaller companies need a rapidly growing economy to help fuel their growth. In the 1970s that steam engine was the United States. But now the tides have turned and the fastest growing consumer markets are now China and India.

China and India are currently growing at a rate 4 times that of developed countries. So even if they slow down some they will likely become high-income regions within the next 15 to 20 years.

Herein lies the problem for small-cap American companies. The majority of these companies is excluded from the emerging markets of China and India and must depend on the slow growth of the U.S. economy. This gives them a rather large disadvantage, which means they are highly unlikely to outperform the large-caps this time.

So I would say avoid these stocks at all costs or they may end up costing you more than you bargained for.

CHAPTER 8

Let the Good Times Roll

We have already shared the doom and gloom of what could happen in the days ahead, but I am sure you are tired of that by now. For those of you that have stuck with me this long you will be rewarded in the coming chapters.

In the previous chapter we talked about investments that were deemed safe in the 1970s but performed rather poorly. Just as there were investments that performed poorly there were investments that did very well. That is going to be the focus of this chapter.

These investments tend to outperform as a result of inflation and energy cost increases. In the 1990s many people stayed away from these investments because the tech sector of the stock market was so hot. Times have changed though and now investments that are some of the most widely owned will begin to shine once again.

The first of these investments is gold. Take a look at the table below and see for yourself the staggering results of gold and gold bullion performance during the inflation of the 1970s.

**Table 6* How Gold Stocks and Gold
Bullion Performed in the 1970s**

	Average annual nominal return	Average annual real return	Total real return	Change in real $10,000
Gold stocks	28.0%	20.6%	550.8%	$65,080
Gold bullion	33.1%	25.7%	884.8%	$94,480

In fact this bull run of gold in the 1970s is the greatest bull run of any single investment in living memory. The stock market did not even do this well in the 1990s during the heavy tech boom.

The reason is quite simple. When everything is stable in the economy and things are growing, financial assets are what everyone is buying. However, when the times get tough gold is one of the few investments that you will want to bank on.

Gold is one of the greatest hedges against inflation. The reason behind this is that the government is not just able to create more gold at any given time like it can paper or electronic dollars. So as the value of the dollar falls, the price of gold rises.

This is why gold is the number one inflation hedge. During the period of the 1970s and other inflationary periods it is one of the only investments able to keep up with rising prices.

Before 1975 the price of gold was fixed at $35 per ounce, but in 1975 it began trading freely at $200 an ounce. By early 1980 gold reached it's all time high of $850. In real terms that equates to a 10 fold increase in value.

Likewise gold-mining companies had an impressive run in the 1970s. If you would have invested in the gold stock index of the S&P 500 you would have made 18 times on your money. It averages to about 37.5 percent per year, which is far better than the tech stock index of the NASDAQ did in the 1990s.

Of course in the '90s gold suffered horrible losses reaching a low of $250 an ounce in 1999. Remember we explained that this happens because the vogue turned towards the stock market due to the expectation of a good economic future. The picture is much bleaker today.

That is why in recent years gold has had another bull run that reached $730 an ounce in May of 2006. We have obviously entered a new uptrend, which I believe will continue and will eventually reach more than $1000 an ounce. Still most investors see gold as something barbaric and outdated.

Unfortunately this is a prime example of people following the trend set by mass psychology. Since the '90s is so fresh in many investors minds they will miss out on another "golden opportunity."

Once advisors begin to see a definite trend of inflation they will begin to advise their clients to move 5-10 percent of their assets into inflation hedges. This one move alone will drive gold prices through the roof.

If a bull market in gold does return like the one in the 1970s, most gold shares will do well. But I will add that you should beware of the new companies that jump on the scene during this time. Their prices may overshoot the value, which could be a similar situation to the tech boom of the 90s. Stick with the big producers.

Black Gold
How Oil and Oil Stocks Performed in the 1970s

Investment	Average annual nominal returns	Average annual real returns	Total real returns	Change in real $10,000
Crude Oil	26.4%	19.0%	469.5%	$56,950
Oil Service Companies	31.0%	23.6%	732.1%	$83,210
Big Oil Companies	14.2%	6.8%	93.1%	$19,310
Independent Oil Producers	19.2%	23.6%	732.1%	$83,210

As you already know by reading the section of the book about the oil crisis we are possibly facing we could very well see continuing significant increases in the price of oil over the next 10 years. If you look back in history you will see that the crude oil prices rose considerably during the 1970s. In the last three years the price of oil has more than doubled. Due to the underlying fundamentals I am convinced that this bull market in energy will last longer and reach prices that are considerably higher than any other we have ever seen.

So how do you invest in this market? Well, unlike gold bullion you cannot purchase crude oil and store it in a safe until you are ready to sell it. If you trade oil futures contracts you need to develop some specialized knowledge of the market, which requires a lot of time. So what do most investors do? They invest in oil companies. And just like gold, oil stocks are extremely undervalued at the moment.

The buzz on the Street right now is that oil will trade somewhere between $25 and $45 a barrel within 3 years' time. However during 2005 oil traded consistently at more than $60 a barrel.

As a result of Wall Street's perception of the future market, oil shares are priced at a level that assumes $30 oil. What does this mean for you, the investor? It means that there is big potential as the oil shares increase to catch up with the continued high price of oil. You mix that with the oil crunch that I believe we are facing and you have yourself a bundle of profit.

As seen by the above table, all sectors in the oil industry did very well during the 70s. I believe this will ring true again in the next 5 to 10 years.

CHAPTER 9

The Next Hot Investment: Currencies

When people ask me what I do and I say, "I am a currency trader," they often have a confused look on their faces. They think of the person sitting behind the window at an airport exchanging one currency for another. In fact I find that most of my clients did not know what foreign exchange investing was before they found me. So for those of you that don't know let me give you a history of events that brought the world's largest market into existence.

The Bretton Woods Era

In July of 1944, representatives of 44 nations met in Bretton Woods, New Hampshire, to create a new institutional arrangement for governing the international economy in the years after World War II. Most agreed that the reason for the war was economic instability, which needed to be prevented in the future.

The planners at Bretton Woods established the International Bank for Reconstruction and Development (IBRD), now one of five institutions in the World Bank Group; the International

Monetary Fund (IMF); and the General Agreement on Tariffs and trade. These organizations became operational in 1946 after a sufficient number of countries had ratified the agreement, and they are all still in existence today and play a crucial role in the development and regulation of international economies. It was the IMF that initially enforced the price of $35 per ounce for gold, which was to be fixed under the Bretton Woods system.

So what did this key agreement consist of? There were actually a few key points.

1. The formation of key international authorities (like the ones above) to promote fair trade and international economic harmony.
2. The fixing of exchange rates among currencies.
3. The convertability between gold and the U.S. dollar, thus empowering the U.S. dollar as the reserve currency of choice for the world.

Of the three parameters only the first is still in existence today.

The Bretton Woods agreement was in operation from 1944 to 1971, at which time it was replaced with the Smithsonian Agreement. This agreement was spearheaded by U.S. President Richard Nixon, and was not any better than the Bretton Woods Agreement. The downfall was that it maintained fixed exchange rates, which did not accommodate the ongoing U.S. trade deficit and the international need for a weaker dollar.

Eventually, we had to evolve into a free market world economy that is dominated by supply and demand, which determine the value of a currency. This allows the markets to self regulate, which enables the market to dictate the appropriate value of a currency without any hindrances.

If nothing more, Bretton Woods established the U.S. dollar as the dominant world currency, even though the British Pound is still much stronger and the Euro is a trailblazer for both social behavior and international trade. By establishing dollar/gold convertibility, the Bretton Woods agreement fortified its role as the most reliable and accessible currency.

The End of Bretton Woods

After the Bretton Woods Accord came the Smithsonian Agreement in December of 1971. This agreement was similar to the Bretton Woods Accord, but allowed for a greater fluctuation band for the currencies. In 1972, the European community tried to move away from its dependency on the dollar. West Germany, France, Italy, the Netherlands, Belgium and Luxembourg established the European Joint Float. The agreement was similar to the Bretton Woods Accord, but allowed a greater range of fluctuation in the currency values.

Both agreements made mistakes similar to the Bretton Woods Accord and collapsed in 1973. As a result the foreign exchange markets were forced to close from February of 1972 to March of 1973 when they were reopened. The collapse of the Smithsonian agreement and the European Joint Float in 1973 signified the official switch to the free-floating system. This occurred by default, as there were no new agreements to take their place. Governments were now free to peg their currencies, semi-peg or allow them to freely float. In 1978, the free-floating system was officially mandated.

Devaluation of the Dollar

By the late 1970s every exchange rate regulatory system that had been set up in the twentieth century had failed. These included the gold standard, the Bretton Woods Agreement, and the Smithsonian Agreement. So the only way for the currency market to operate was based upon free market capitalism where supply and demand ruled the market. However there was a problem with this particular way of operation by which the currency markets were regulated. This was revealed when unforeseen economic events occurred such as the development of the OPEC oil crisis, stagflation during the 1970s, and drastic changes in the Federal Reserve's fiscal policy.

The system that was developed was more flexible than the other systems that had hindered the stability of the currency markets throughout the twentieth century. And so in 1985 a definite solution was developed. The world's leading economies – the United States, France Germany, Japan, and the United Kingdom – met in New York city at the Plaza Hotel in hopes of developing a system that would solve the economic ineffectiveness of the foreign exchange markets. The plan had to be comprised of agreements that would shape the global economy as well as specific economies that were involved.

At the time, most of the world was experiencing low levels of inflation and strong growth. This caused some imbalances in the major world economies such as the United States, Germany, and Japan. Germany and Japan had large and growing surpluses while the United States was experiencing large and growing deficits. The leaders were trying to protect against a disruption in the equilibrium of the foreign currency markets knowing that it would lead to a distortion of international economies.

Many believed this imbalance was due to the accelerated appreciation of the U.S. dollar to the currencies of its major trading partners. The inflated dollar valuation meant that the exporting and importing capabilities of other countries was severely affected. Thus a lower dollar would promote stability in the international economy.

So at the Plaza Hotel, on September 22, 1985, the Plaza Accord was put into action. It was essentially an intervention in which each country represented agreed to do certain individual things.

Each country agreed to intervene when necessary in order to get the value of the dollar down. The United States' role was to cut its budget deficit and lower interest rates. France, the United Kingdom, Japan, and Germany all agreed to raise interest rates. The problems with this agreement arose when the countries involved did not strictly adhere to their intentions. Japan was required to let the yen "fully reflect the underlying strength of its economy." They of course did this, but the United States did not follow through on their promise to cut the budget deficit. As a result the Japanese economy suffered incredibly by the strong rise in the yen. This caused its exporters to be unable to remain competitive overseas. Many believe this is what caused the recession that Japan suffered for more than 10 years. The United States on the other hand benefited from the agreement and enjoyed strong growth and price stability.

The agreement did work in resolving the imbalance between the U.S. dollar and other major world currencies. Within 2 years the U.S. dollar had 46% and 50% against the deutsche mark and the Japanese yen, respectively. During this time the U.S. adapted to become far more export-oriented while the other nations such as Germany and Japan became import-oriented. This solved the current account deficit for a period of time. However the more important development was that the central banks became the major determinates in regulating exchange rate movement. This meant that the rates would not be fixed and would be determined by supply and demand. It became the right and the responsibility of the central banks to intervene on behalf of the international economy when necessary.

Major Crisis Spells Big Profits

One of the greatest benefits to being invested in the foreign exchange market is the fact that you can trade and make profits in both bull and bear markets. This is perfect for times when there is high economic uncertainty and potential for great crisis. Never before has there been a time when there is more of both of these factors. This is why I believe that the Foreign Currency market is one of the greatest untapped potentials for many investors. The key is to understand certain events around the globe and anticipate how they will effect the economies of the world.

I would like to show you just a few of the times throughout the history of this market when great profits were realized. Undeniably every opportunity was preceded by a major crisis. For example let's take a look at the time George Soros capitalized on the United Kingdom's decision to join the ERM (Exchange Rate Mechanism).

In 1979 France and Germany initiated an agreement that set up the European Monetary System (EMS). The primary purpose of the EMS was to stabilize exchange rates, reduce inflation, and prepare for monetary integration. The ERM was a main element of the EMS. The way it worked is that each participatory currency was given a central exchange rate against a basket of other currencies called the ECU (European Currency Unit). The participatory currencies were then required to maintain exchange rates within a 2.25 percent fluctuation band above or below each bilateral central rate. Even though the United Kingdom was not one of the original currencies to join it would eventually do so in 1990.

Problems began to be created for the ERM when Germany reunified in 1989 causing government spending to soar. This increased spending led to the Bundesbank grudgingly having to print more money. Of course we know that when you print more money inflation goes up which is a chain reaction for interest rates to go up. This had significant repercussions on the German mark and other currencies involved in the ERM. The German mark was being bombarded with constant upward pressure, which meant that the other currencies' central banks had to raise their interest rates as well. George Soros capitalized on this opportunity knowing that the United Kingdom's weak economy and high unemployment rate could not maintain this constant upward pressure.

If you don't know who George Soros is you can type his name in on Google and you will find out rather quickly. In short he is the fund manager for the Quantum Hedge Fund and he is also known as the man who broke the Bank of England. What he did was simply speculate that the pound would depreciate based upon them either devaluing the pound or leaving the ERM. So the action he took was to establish short positions in pounds and long positions in marks by borrowing pounds and investing in mark-denominated assets. Of course Soros was not the only one and shortly after he took his nearly $10 billion dollar position others followed suit. The pound was feeling extreme downward pressure, which would result in a tug of war between the Bank of England and the speculators.

The initial response of the Bank of England was to defend its pegged rate by buying 15 billion pounds using its large reserve assets. Its intervention was powerless. On September 16, 1992, a day that would later be deemed Black Wednesday, the bank made another flailing attempt to salvage its position by raising interest rates by 2 percent from 10 percent to 12 percent. This was done in order to try and drive investors by boosting the pound's appeal. The speculators, including Soros, did not budge. By the end of the day the move forced Britain to leave the ERM and lower their rates to the previous levels. This day marked a long and steep depreciation of the pound's value.

Over the next 5 weeks the pound depreciated over 15 percent against the deutsche mark and 25 percent against the U.S. dollar. As a result Soros and the other traders banked enormous profits. In one month's time George Soros and his Quantum Fund had cashed in on over $2 billion worth of profits.

Then there was the Asian Market financial crash of 1997 and 1998. Caused by major fundamental breakdowns, the event rocked the Asian currencies. The breakdown spread like a wild fire that came ablaze by obscure lending practices, inflated trade deficits, and unstable capital markets. The discombobulated state of the region debilitated many currencies that were once highly valued and rendered them worthless. What happened next was an unbelievable opportunity for profit in the Asian foreign exchange markets.

The problems for Japan began in the early '90s and materialized into a full-blown crisis by 1997. In 1994 Japan announced a $136 billion total in questionable and non-performing loans, but by the next year the figure climbed to an outstanding $400 billion. This, along with a weak stock market, depreciating real estate values, and a cooling off of the economy, drove investors to put selling pressure on the yen. When the house of cards finally collapsed, Japan's asset prices fell by nearly 10 trillion dollars. Real estate prices alone accounted for nearly 65 percent of the $10 trillion decline. This decline in assets set in motion one of the worst banking crises we have seen in living memory. The collapse of the financial system of Japan also caused investors to put heavy selling pressure on neighboring currencies such as the Thai bat and the Indonesian rupiah.

Today, Asia's economies are full steam ahead once again. They have begun to rebuild their status among the world's industrialized economic regions, only this time they are doing it with more experience in the foreign exchange market than ever before. One way they are doing this is to make sure they have large amounts of reserves to fight against an attack by speculators on their currencies.

The EURO

The introduction of the euro was one of the greatest economic achievements of modern history. It was officially launched as an electronic trading currency on January 1, 1999. That date was one for the history books as the euro marked the beginning of the largest monetary changeover ever. Germany, France, Spain, Ireland, Luxembourg, the Netherlands, Austria, Portugal, Finland, and Belgium were the initial 11 states that comprised the European Monetary Union also known as the EMU. The United Kingdom, Sweden, Denmark, and Greece decided to keep their own currencies for the time being, but Greece ended up joining two years later. Each currency had to weigh the benefits against the challenges that could arise from joining the EMU. Each currency that joined fixed its currency to a specific conversion rate against the euro. The ECB was made the governing entity of the monetary policy that was adopted and each country was required to align with these policies.

Of course the most noticeable benefit for the citizens of a nation that makes the decision to join the EMU is ease of travel from one state to another. Although this is important there are numerous other benefits that include:

1. The elimination of exchange rate fluctuations. This provides a very stable environment to trade within the euro area.
2. The elimination of transaction costs relating to international business, such as foreign exchange operations, cross-border payments, and hedging operations.
3. The one single currency market, which is very large, attracts foreign investors (Warren Buffet and Bill Gates are two of the many that have invested heavily in the euro).
4. It eliminates exchange rate risk within its zone, which allows businesses to strategize more accurately when it comes to their investment decisions.
5. It increases competition as prices become more transparent, as consumers and businesses can compare prices across countries with greater ease.
6. Due to the size and stability of the economy the ECB is able to more easily control inflation using lower interest rates.

These are just some of the many benefits to joining the Euro, but to every positive there is a negative. The greatest of these negative factors is without a doubt the fact that each participating state must forfeit any independent monetary system. This has the potential to present problems for the countries that are involved, especially the smaller ones. The problem arises in that not every country's economy is a perfect fit, nor are they all directly correlated to the EMU's economy. For instance if a country who is a part of the EMU is experiencing an economic recession at the same time the ECB is hiking interest rates, the country could fall further into recession.

As seen in the chart below, there have been several incredible opportunities for profit on the euro since its inception in 1999. It has gained 32 percent on the dollar since 2001.

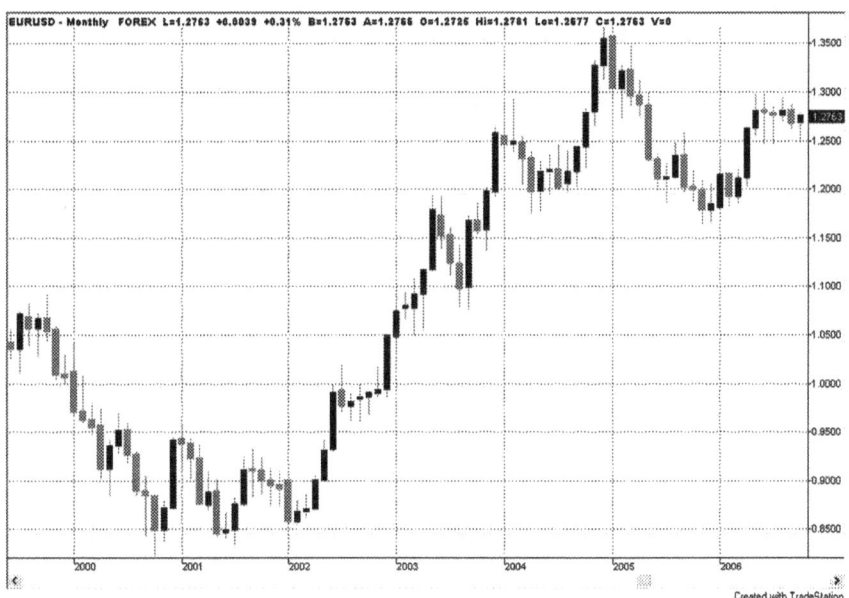

EURUSD showing 32% gains on the dollar

So why do I think that currencies are going to be a hot commodity in the next few years? Historically speaking, any time there is a currency crisis the markets must adjust. In other words they must move significantly. As an investor that is when you either make or lose money.

Here is the big difference between the market of the past and the present day market: in 1973 only the big players could capitalize on the opportunities presented in the foreign exchange market. In fact up until 1997 it was a playground for banks, institutions, large international corporations, and individuals with extreme wealth. The trade size was $1,000,000 and the leverage that is now available was not available then.

Now, with the advent of the Internet and online brokers the opportunity to trade the foreign exchange markets of the world has opened up to the individual investor.

There are several key benefits to this market:

1. It is the largest market in the world (reduces costs of trading).
2. It is a 24-hour a day, 5 day a week market (money works longer).
3. It trends better than stocks (trends are where money is made).
4. It is less volatile than stocks, therefore less risky (averages 1% per day range).
5. It affords greater "leverage" than Stocks (100-1 vs. 2-1).
6. Investment Gains are taxed at a much lower tax rate than Stocks.
7. It has no correlation to the Stock Market, and is much less emotion-driven than the Stock Market, reducing your overall portfolio risk.

FOREX

The World's Largest Market

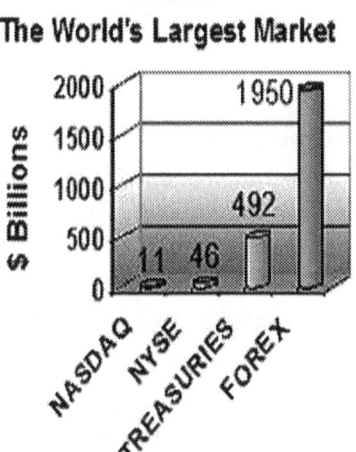

Volume of the Forex Market compared to other markets

The foreign exchange market has a volume of over $1.5 trillion per day making it by far the largest market in the world. What does this mean for you, the investor? This means that you have more of an opportunity to capture profits from your investments. The high liquidity of this market makes it easy to get in and out of the market in the case of a sudden event or crisis.

For example on September 11, 2001 in the attack on the World Trade Center buildings, the market only moved by 350 ticks. So if you had $100,000 invested with proper money management rules in place, and you were in the opposite direction of the move, and you held it for 2 weeks after the news came out you would have suffered a temporary loss of $7,000. This is an unlikely scenario when trading the Forex. That is much better than how some people's portfolios fared during the tech crash of 2000. If you were long on the dollar (long is another term for believing the dollar is going to appreciate) at this point in time you would have had a much closer stop in place which would have immediately taken you out of the market. Then you could have changed your position and gone short on the dollar (short is another term for believing the dollar is going to depreciate).

Why You Need to Invest in Currencies During the Coming Crisis

If you remember in the previous chapter we talked about the bull run of the 1970s that took place in the Gold and Oil sectors. There were phenomenal gains made during this time. But what many people don't know is that the currency market fared just as well.

For instance from 1973 to 1982 if you would have just had one currency pair in your portfolio and left it in and never touched it or added to it you would have seen a real gain of 733%. And there were seven other pairs that fared just like it. Why? Because currencies move during inflationary periods.

In fact the 1970s were great for currencies because currencies love to trend. In the '70s when inflation was high that is exactly what they did. This time around it will be different however. This is because during times of inflation interest rates are driven up in order to cool things back down, but now we cannot drive interest rates up too far. The economy is not strong enough to handle interest rates at high levels. We will have a crisis on our hands. Add this to the fact that we continue to print more and more money and send it in to the world and we are going to see the greatest bear run the dollar has ever seen.

From 1999 to 2001 the dollar was very strong against the euro, which was a situation primarily driven by the U.S. Internet and equity market boom. This caused investors to want to participate in these elevated returns, which in turn caused the country to be flooded with money. Foreign investors were dumping the reserves they held in their own currencies and buying dollars.

Then at the end of 2001 when geopolitical uncertainties arose, the United States started cutting interest rates and foreign investors began to sell U.S. assets in search of higher yields elsewhere. This of course led to foreign investors selling U.S. dollars, increasing supply and lowering the dollar's value against other major currencies.

Since then we have put even more dollars into circulation, which has caused a greater supply of U.S. dollars. When all of the things diverge that we have talked about in this book such as debt, the low savings rate, housing defaults, trade deficits, etc., there will be a massive collapse of the dollar. Foreign investors will begin to pull out of our currency like crazy.

What Moves the Currency Markets?

Like other investments, the currency markets can be looked at in two ways: short-term or long-term. First off let me tell you how I define long- and short- term in the currency market. Long-term is anything more than 2 years. Short-term is anything less than 2 years.

Most investors use the buy and hold strategies when it comes to their retirement accounts. This is normal, especially in investments like mutual funds or stock indexes. The reason is that these investments do not afford the greatest opportunities to trade both ways due to the up tick rule and to the fact that they may not be very liquid. However this is not true for the currency market. Due to the sheer size of the currency market it is very liquid, making it easy to exit and enter the market. This allows for instant and efficient execution of your orders.

The buy and hold strategy is not always the best strategy for the currency market. Since it is so easy to enter and exit positions you are able to take advantage of the movement of the markets. No market trends perfectly up or down. The market moves in waves. The advantage to trading the currency market more short-term is the ability to follow the waves of the market. This produces greater profit potential.

There are ways to trade the currency market long-term also. The long-term approach uses a fundamental technique and requires you to have an in-depth knowledge of national as well as international economies. News about certain economic indicators or events is what moves the market long-term. As seen in the financial crisis of Asia, the market trended down for a solid two and one-half years. Most long-term currency investors use fundamental analysis to determine a currency's correct valuation as well as its future valuation.

Investors who use fundamental analysis must focus on the economic, social, and political forces at work in each nation of the currency they are trading. The moving forces in fundamental analysis are indicators that focus on supply and demand. The less supply and more demand there is for a certain currency the more that currency is going to be worth. Hence, the more supply of a currency there is the less it will be worth. This is why the statement made by the current Federal Reserve Chairman Ben Bernanke when he said the U.S. would print as much money as they needed is so scary. It was said once that during the Cold War there were more $100 bills in Russia than there were in the U.S. We have been sending our money overseas for so long there is no telling how much of a supply there is. That is why when the demand for U.S. dollars begins to fall off, the dollar will plummet. This is an example of how fundamental analysis works, only we use economic indicators to help us foresee the reaction of the market in a specific unit of time and price movement.

Fundamental analysis of currencies is done by looking at different macroeconomic indicators such as interest rates, growth rates, inflation, and unemployment. This method requires a great deal of focus and dedication, but it can be very accurate in determining trend direction. Investors using this method to trade currencies must be aware of news that comes out on a daily, weekly, monthly, and quarterly basis. A fundamental trader knows when key announcements or key events are taking place. Events such as G7 or G8 finance meetings, presidential elections, important summits, major central bank meetings, potential changes to currency regimes, and possible debt defaults by large countries, are all known as big events.

For the short-term fundamental trader, also known as day traders, there are several major news announcements that are released every month from several different countries that have the potential to move the market significantly. The major U.S. news announcements are Non-Farm Payrolls, FOMC rate decisions, Trade Balance, CPI (inflation report), Retail Sales, GDP, Current Account, Durable Goods, and TIC data. The fundamental day trader must pay close attention to these announcements, as they will give signals for trading opportunities. Analyzing past data to determine which variations of future numbers will give the best opportunity is the fundamental trader's primary focus.

The next type of analysis used for determining trends and entry and exit points of a specific trade is called technical analysis. There has been a long-running competition going on between technical and fundamental traders. The winner of the battle has never really been determined because they both have pros and cons. Personally I believe the best type of trading system uses a mix of fundamental and technical analysis. The major benefit to the technical trader is the ease to apply technical strategies to a broad range of currencies. The fundamental trader does not have this advantage, as they must rigorously study many aspects of an economy in order to have enough information to make a trading decision.

The best mix is to use fundamental data to determine the future trend of currency pairs and use technical analysis to trade within that trend. I have found that this approach works exceptionally well because the currency market trends very strong. The technical trader should be aware of key economic, social and political news because these fundamentals have the potential to trigger breakouts or trend reversals.

The style of analysis that you feel most comfortable with will determine the amount of time you must spend analyzing the markets. One of the greatest benefits of trading the foreign exchange market is that you have the opportunity to trade at various times throughout the day. The Asian markets open at 7 p.m. CST followed by the European at 2 a.m. CST and lastly New York opens at 7:30 a.m. CST. This allows you greater flexibility of your time depending on where you are in the world or what your schedule is like. This flexibility coupled with the development of online trading platforms for the individual investor may be one reason that there has been such a surge in volume over the last few years. In September of 2004 the Bank for International Settlements, which publishes the Triennial Central Bank Survey, stated that daily trading volume hit a record high of $1.9 trillion, up from $1.2 trillion in 2001. This is roughly 20 times the daily trading volume of the New York Stock Exchange and the NASDAQ combined.

So why is the size of the FX market so enormous? Well, if you remember at the beginning of this chapter I discussed that the FX market used to be a big-players-only market. Only those with access to the interbank market were able to tap into this kind of market. This is where only the largest go to profit. On this level banks are trading with banks through Electronic Brokering Services or Reuters. Since the interbank market is a credit-approved system only banks that have established credit relationships with other banks can trade with one another. All other institutions such as hedge funds, FX market makers, and corporations must trade through the FX corporate banks. The banks are able to see all of the other dealing rates in the market. If you take a look at the table below you will see the Bank of America's 2003 & 2004 Trading Related Revenues Report.

2004 Annual Report: Financial Review: Management's Discussion and Analysis: Business Segment Operations

(Dollars in millions)	2004	2003
Net interest income (fully taxable-equivalent basis)	$2,039	$2,239
Trading account profits	1,028	587
Total trading-related revenue	**$3,067**	**$2,826**
Trading-related revenue by product		
Fixed income	$1,547	$1,352
Interest rate (fully taxable-equivalent basis)	667	954
Foreign exchange	757	551
Equities	195	344
Commodities	45	(45)
Market-based trading-related revenue	3,211	3,156
Credit portfolio hedges	(144)	(330)
Total trading-related revenue	**$3,067**	**$2,826**

Bank of America's trade related revenue 2003-2004

As you can see Foreign Exchange is one of their biggest profit earners. The big banks have been riding this wave for years. Because of the fact that you need an established credit line with big banks to receive the rates they are able to offer, institutional investors and corporations are not able to obtain them. However, recent technology has changed the way this operates. The roadblocks between the end user of foreign exchange services and the interbank market have been broken down. Now, retail clients are able to connect with the market makers in a low cost manner. Online trading platform technology now serves as a portal for individual investors to tap into the liquidity of the FX market. Now average traders and investors can ride on the coattails of the big banks and take advantage of the same opportunities. This is why when the stuff hits the fan this market will offer an incredible opportunity to individual investors.

Another reason for great opportunity in this market as the dollar weakens is because as of right now over 90 percent of all currency transactions involve the U.S. dollar. This means that as the dollar crashes the cross pairs will get stronger and will trend longer. This makes for a great opportunity when it comes to investing.

Prior to September 11, 2001 the U.S. dollar was considered the worlds' safe haven currency. Prior to 9/11 the risk of severe instability in the U.S. dollar was very low and the U.S. was one of the most stable and developed economies in the world. This allowed the U.S. to attract investment at a discounted rate of return. This offering resulted in over 76 percent of global currency reserves being held in dollars. Another major reason why currency reserves are largely held in dollars is the fact that the dollar is the world's dominant factoring currency. Due to the dollar's stability pre-9/11 it played a major role for foreign central banks. However, in the years since 9/11 the same foreign investors and central banks that had heavily invested in the dollar have now trimmed off a large portion of their holdings. Now, many of the investors are diversifying into the new major player on the scene, the euro. Numerous central banks have already begun this diversification process into euros by reducing their dollar holdings and increasing their euro holdings. If this trend continues it will become a major determinant for the future of the U.S. dollar.

Tapping Into the Potential of the FX Market

There are many resources that you can get your hands on to learn more about the FX market. I personally have successfully trained over 1500 people to trade the FX market using various techniques. At the back of this book I provide a list of resources for you to invest in if you feel the desire to do so. The learning curve is approximately one year, but could be done in as little as 6 months. On the other hand it may take you 2 years or more to learn the markets good enough to invest successfully on your own. Then again you may never learn the market good enough to become successful. In fact over 90% of traders fail within their first year. I believe the number one reason for this is that they do not stick with it long enough and they do not follow the rules of the system they learn.

Trading the FX market is more than just learning how to read a chart and use certain indicators. It is even more than being able to understand the economies of the world. I know of many economists and analysts who are very brilliant, but they couldn't make a penny in the FX market to save their lives. In fact if you gave them any money to invest they would probably lose it all. I also know of CPAs, lawyers and doctors who are very brilliant at what they do, but they can't trade to save their lives. Trading is a different animal. In fact I have found that most overachievers do not do well at the markets at all. The main reason for this I believe is due to the simple fact that you cannot beat the market. If you try it will beat your brains out. It is bigger than you and it is a beast. You have to learn how to flow with the market. Overachievers do not like this. They always want to conquer. The problem is you cannot conquer this market. Therefore most people who are very good at their current professions do not do well in the FX market. There are exceptions, but they are very few and far between.

By now I am sure you are saying to yourself, "Gosh, I like what I am hearing but it sounds complicated." Well, let me say that I am not trying to get you to think that you can't do it. I want you to succeed in your investments and that was my purpose for writing this book, but you must understand that you will have to devote yourself to learning before you try to invest or you need to invest in an FX fund. The bottom line is that there is no such thing as success without sacrifice. So before you begin to trade on your own make sure that you are going to finish what you start. Make sure you have a good plan of action before you start.

FX funds are a good place to start while you learn. However, you need to be careful who you choose for this, as there are many bad investors out there. Make sure they have outside CPA compiled reports. The big players like Janus, Charles Schwab and others are not going to offer high yielding FX investments. You will need an FX fund manager to invest this portion of your portfolio. I would also recommend no more than 35% diversification into this investment or any other for that matter. You need to find someone with a short-term and medium-term trading style. This would be a blend of day and swing trading. Realistically you should be able to achieve 40 percent gains or more on your FX investment annually.

The following charts show you what a $100,000 FX fund investment would turn into after 10 years of compounded 40 percent average returns.

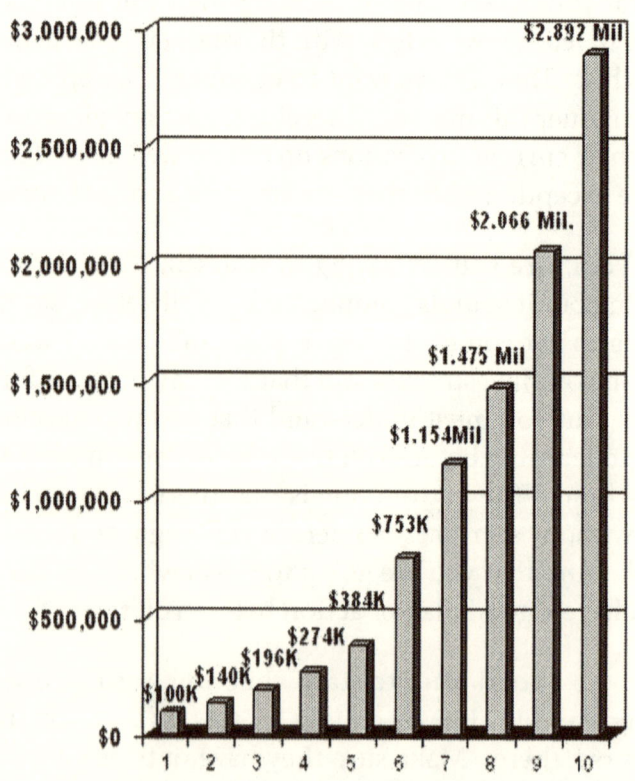

Forex Investment over 10 years

In 10 years you would have over $2.8 million. That is a nice retirement. These are the kind of returns that have been seen by the market makers and banks for years. The average middle to upper middle class citizen could retire on that amount of money and live very comfortably.

Another great advantage to the FX market is that you are allowed to roll your IRA or 401(k) account into this type of investment in order to maintain tax deferred growth. This gives you the ability to move some of your retirement funds that have not been producing very well into a market that has done exceptionally well in recent history. Of course there are many tax strategies when it comes to investing and if you have a good CPA you can get all of the tax advice you need from them.

I believe there are two types of people in this world. There are those that have their future determined for them and those that determine their own future. You can see this all throughout our society. One major difference between these two types of people is the fact that the ones who determine their own future are people that are willing to do whatever it takes (legally and morally) to get what they need to become successful. These are people who are willing to invest in themselves. They're people who aren't afraid to step out into new territory. If you have completed this book I believe you are one of these types of people. You are a trendsetter. Also known as someone who is willing to challenge the ideologies of the masses. If you truly are there is no doubt you will become successful in your investments.

Knowledge is power. That is why you must gain the knowledge you need to become good at investing, or you need to get around others that have the knowledge, and I'm not talking about your next door neighbor who gave you a hot stock tip. That is why I have compiled a list of books and other resources that you will find very useful in your pursuit of profitable investing. I also challenge you to research out the ideas and thoughts of this book yourself.

I personally believe what I have written in this book to be sound advice. That is why I follow it. That's right, I practice what I preach. I am invested in oil, gold and the FX markets. The majority of my personal investment is in the FX market because this is what I specialize in. I study these markets on a daily basis. I study the economies of the world. That is what I love to do. It is my passion. I encourage you to become passionate and proactive about your investments also. This is the only way you will achieve your financial goals.

I believe when you see my track record you will agree that it is above average. But I do have one drawback: I do not accept smaller investors. I never have and I never will. It's nothing personal, it's just that I enjoy working with and trading for only certain types of clients. Please see www.forexassetgroup.com for the current minimum and performance. Even if you don't invest I encourage you to sign up for my free newsletter to keep you up to date on the oil, gold and currency markets.

You're funds are always liquid and there is no penalty to add or withdraw funds at any time. The most important thing (next to superior returns) is that unlike mutual fund and other managers who get paid a management fee, I charge a performance fee. To get paid 1-2% a year in management fees whether the client made money or not really isn't fair, that is why I don't charge one. Many traditional investment advisors don't like it when I expose that fact. They almost all recommend diversification but usually only into stocks and bonds. So if the whole market tanks are you really diversified? Of course not. True diversification includes real estate, oil, gold, and currencies. I believe adding a currency fund to your portfolio will increase your risk-adjusted returns.

If you do want to pay the price and learn to trade I also offer a training course at www.4xeducator.com Instead of me describing it here just take a few minutes to read my homepage. Thank you for taking the time to read this book and I wish you the best with your investments. God Bless.

FOREX INVESTMENTS LP TRADING SYSTEM OVERVIEW & PHILOSOPHY

Forex Investments LP believes in capital preservation first and profits second. Mr. Robles' fundamental approach to the spot foreign currency market is to be risk averse. Capital preservation is much more important to portfolio growth than capturing every possible opportunity that presents itself.

Mr. Robles has designed a trading system to recognize conditions wherein the underlying market is in a state of accumulation or distribution of one currency relative to another. Once the market direction has been determined, trades are placed based on price relationship to support and resistance levels and the probability that the trend will continue. Trend line breaks is one of the best ways to determine trend direction, momentum and high probability trades. Mr. Robles also does contrarian trades when price level are extremely overbought or oversold.

The system relies on modifications to existing technical indicators such as MACD and Stochastics, the development of proprietary indicators, and the use of technical pivot points and support/resistance levels. Through a correlation of these variables, Mr. Robles has developed a system where these trends can be identified and exploited. The entry and exit signals are evaluated against the macro analysis and examination of the overall market. The combination of a statistical signal and a subjective review results in a system which is not black box, but discretionary.

Risk management and trade discipline are the cornerstones of Forex Investments' trading philosophy. Adhering to strict risk management guidelines and applying a disciplined approach to the trading system is always applied. The use of hedging is one of Mr. Robles best approaches for doing this.

Mr. Robles also performs fundamental analysis by looking at the economic conditions that affect the valuation of a nation's currency relative to other currencies. Mr. Robles will monitor periodic economic calendar events and economic reports of relevant countries. In cases when non-scheduled news, comments or events occur, Mr. Robles will collectively analyze those events to see if these news releases from government agencies is really an economic event or just a public relations vehicle to advance a particular point of view or policy. The trading program has a hedging strategy to counter any catastrophic events.

The trading plan is continuously monitored, re-tested, and examined to determine whether or not it continues to be relevant to changing macro market conditions.

Mr. Robles also has taught over 1,500 individual and institutional traders how to trade with his patent pending Fundamental Traders course which can be found at: www.4xeducator.com

Forex Investments LP
2800 W. Main Suite C, League City TX 77573
info@forexassetgroup.com
www.forexassetgroup.com
www.4xeducator.com

U.S. Government Required Disclosure - Commodity Futures Trading Commission. Forex, Futures and options trading has large potential rewards, but also large potential risk. You must be aware of the risks and be willing to accept them in order to invest in the futures and options markets. Don't trade with money you can't afford to lose. This website is neither a solicitation nor an offer to Buy/Sell futures or options. No representation is being made that any account will or is likely to achieve profits or losses similar to those discussed on the website. The past performance of any trading system or methodology is not necessarily indicative of future results.

References

What Has Government Done to Our Money?
Rothbard, Murray N.
1963, 1985, 1990
Praxeology Press, Ludwig Von Mises Institute, Auburn University,
Auburn, AL

The Second Great Depression
Brussee, Warren
2005
Booklocker.com, Inc.

Conquer the Crash: You Can Survive and Prosper in a Deflationary
Depression
Prechter, Robert R, Jr.
2002
John Wiley & Sons, Inc., Hoboken, NJ

The Coming Collapse of the Dollar and How to Profit From It:
Make a Fortune by Investing in Gold and Other Hard Assets
Rubino, John and Turk, James
2004

A Currency Book Published by Doubleday, a Division of Random House, Inc.

The Coming Economic Collapse: How You Can Thrive When Oil Costs $200 a Barrel
Leeb, Stephen, PhD, with Glen C. Strathy
2006
Warner Business Books, Warner Books, Time Warner Book Group, New York, NY

The Dollar Crisis: Causes, Consequences, Cures
Duncan, Richard
2005
John Wiley & Sons (Asia) Pte Ltd, Singapore

The Chastening: Inside the Crisis that Rocked the Global Financial System and Humbled the IMF
Blustein, Paul
2001, 2003
Public Affairs, a member of the Perseus Books Group, Cambridge, MA

The Demise of the Dollar . . . and Why It's Great for Your Investments
Wiggin, Addison
2005
John Wiley & Sons, Inc, Hoboken, NJ

Empire of Debt: The Rise of an Epic Financial Crisis
Bonner, William and Wiggin, Addison
2006
John Wiley & Sons, Inc, Hoboken, NJ

The Oil Factor: Protect Yourself—and Profit—from the Coming Energy Crisis
Leeb, Stephen and Leeb, Donna
2004
Warner Business Books, Warner Books, Time Warner Book Group, New York, NY

About the Author

Forex Investments LP believes in capital preservation first and profits second. Mr. Robles' fundamental approach to the spot foreign currency market is to be risk averse. Capital preservation is much more important to portfolio growth than capturing every possible opportunity that presents itself. Mr. Robles has designed a trading system to recognize conditions wherein the underlying market is in a state of accumulation or distribution of one currency relative to another. Once the market direction has been determined, trades are placed based on price relationship to support and resistance levels and the probability that the trend will continue. The system relies on modifications to existing technical indicators such as MACD and Stochastics, the development of proprietary indicators, and the use of technical pivot points and support/resistance levels. Through a correlation of these variables, Mr. Robles has developed a system where these trends can be identified and exploited. The entry and exit signals are evaluated against the macro analysis and examination of the overall market. The combination of a statistical signal and a subjective review results in a system which is not black box, but discretionary. Risk management and trade discipline are the cornerstones of Forex Investments' trading philosophy. Adhering to strict risk management guidelines and applying a disciplined approach to the trading system is always applied. The use of hedging is one of Mr. Robles best approaches for doing this. Mr. Robles also performs fundamental analysis by looking at the economic conditions that affect the valuation of a nation's currency relative to other currencies. The trading program has a hedging strategy to counter any catastrophic events. The trading plan is continuously monitored, re-tested, and examined to determine whether or not it continues to be relevant to changing macro market conditions.